D0358782

'Gripping, heart-breaking, challenging – this memoir about a family in crisis is a must-read.'
Sophie Hannah

This is Joanne's account of coming to terms with her brother's suicide and through that process, the entirety of her family life. In *Small Pieces* Joanne explores her childhood, her Jewishness and her mother's death as well as that of her brother.

The life and family described is a complex combination of conflicting influences – both scientific and literary; Jewish and humanist impulses; and middle American and North London settings.

Small Pieces is a beautiful and searingly honest meditation on family and faith.

'Weighs the peculiar burdens and joys of family and faith with startling insight and humour.'
Marina Benjamin, author of *The Middlepause*

4 1 0284101 4

Small Pieces

Also by Joanne Limburg

Femenismo

Paraphernalia

The Woman Who Thought Too Much

The Oxygen Man

Bookside Down

A Want of Kindness

The Autistic Alice

Small Pieces

A Book of Lamentations

Joanne Limburg

Atlantic Books
London

Published in hardback in Great Britain in 2017 by Atlantic Books,
an imprint of Atlantic Books Ltd.

10 9 8 7 6 5 4 3 2 1

A CIP catalogue record for this book is available from the British Library.

Hardback ISBN: 978 1 78649 230 2
E-book ISBN: 978 1 78649 231 9

Printed and bound in Great Britain by Bell and Bain Ltd, Glasgow

Atlantic Books
An Imprint of Atlantic Books Ltd
Ormond House
26–27 Boswell Street
London
WC1N 3JZ

www.atlantic-books.co.uk

To my brother

Author's Note

To protect the privacy of those involved in my family's story, most names have been changed.

Sister

She will harrow this town, she will turn him up,
whole or in pieces. Being a sister,
she knows that brothers are born to trouble.
Her part is to rescue him,
lend him a heart to face his enemies,
or failing that, confound them herself
with withheld smiles, or with her sharp
big sister's tongue; and if she finds
them gone to ground, their damage done,
she'll cut the losses for both of them
and seek him out, wherever he's lying,
broken and say, *Brother, there's*
no shame in one lost battle, or
in ten. Put the phial down –
don't drink! And if it is too late
for that, she'll scruff the man and stick
her fingers down his throat, or find
an antidote, or make her own,
or heave time back, or failing that,
and even failing that, she'll take him home,
and never mind how small the pieces.

I don't take notes

I don't pack a notebook with me, I don't buy one at any of the airports, or in Plainsville. The notes I take are few, scribbled in the front of my address book. Here they are in total:

Diversity

choice

options

share

Please wait while we create a variety of entertainment choices for you.

Psalm #91

In the lab, they culture competent cells.

Ant & Dec

My brother's keeper.

Bluebird of happiness.

Wild turkey.

Buzzsaw cicadas.

deer

lizard

These were my reminders of the strongest impressions, the notes I could not refrain from making – the signs of my writerly incontinence. They were a clear indication, even then, that I would break the vow I had made, not to write about any of this, because to write about this, to make creative or any other kind of capital out of it, would place me so beyond the pale that the only honourable course would be to kill myself in turn.

Rabbis

You need to understand that a great deal of time has passed since the fall of the Temple, so we've had to survive all these centuries without priests and without offerings. We have relied instead on rabbis and on printed words: rabbis are no closer to God than other Jews – God is *broiges* with us,* he won't speak directly any more – but they have studied his old words in greater depth than the rest of us, and for this reason, if nothing else, we bring our questions to them. We have to bring them somewhere.

The worse the situation, the more urgent the question: when you're ill, when someone dies, when jobs are lost and marriages are breaking up, when the discontented among the nations remember that they hate us and start their persecution up again – that's when you go looking for rabbis. Or if you don't, someone else will. After my brother's suicide, my mother and I arrived at his home in the Midwest to discover that an old school friend of his had found a rabbi right there in the middle of the plains and contacted him on our behalf. He wasn't the sort of rabbi we were used to seeing: like my brother's school friend, he was very Orthodox, and we were more accustomed to the Reform variety, but we were dazed, and very much in need, so of course we saw him.

He told us that my brother had a Jewish soul, and right now it was more at peace than it had ever been.

'He didn't deserve what happened to him,' he said. 'We say that when someone dies as he did, that it's not their fault, because

---

* Annoyed or upset with someone. Not on speaking terms.

something has just taken them over. I want to reassure you: he is at peace.'

'What I find so hard,' my mother said, '– one of the many things – was that he'd been cremated before we got here – cremated with no funeral.'

'I know – that must be very hard for you to think about – but it makes no difference to how we see him or his death.'

My mother was all tears. I looked at her, and remembered her crying some eighteen years before, when her Auntie Yetta was cremated at Golders Green. Not only was it forbidden but also – and I think she was watching the smoke coming out of the chimney when she said this – how could any Jew choose to be cremated, after everything that's happened? She didn't say that again this time. She only said that she would have prayers said for my brother when we got home, and the rabbi said that would be the right thing to do. Someone should say Kaddish for my brother, for his Jewish soul.

I saw my mother's tears but I did not feel for her – I could not, for my own protection, and because I was concentrating on feeling for my brother. He was angry, I thought; he was an atheist, he had married out – he would not appreciate having the existence of his soul confirmed, let alone its Jewishness.

'I can see,' the rabbi said, 'that you are both in your way good Jews.'

And then I clenched my Jewish teeth…

But five years later, when I had a question, it was that rabbi I chose to email:

Dear Rabbi _____,

I hope I have reached the right person. I think it was you who spoke to me and my mother after my brother, Julian Limburg, took his own life in Plainsville in 2008.

My mother certainly found your words very comforting. Sadly, she died herself two years ago. As the last member of my nuclear family of origin, it fell to me to arrange her burial, memorial stone and stone consecration. It was some comfort to be able to arrange things as she would have wanted them.

You might remember that my brother was a scientist, but I'm a writer by profession, and writing is how I process my grief. With this in mind, I have been revisiting the conversation we had with you, and I remember your saying that from a Jewish point of view, my brother had done nothing wrong – something had taken him over, you said – but when I look up the subject of Judaism and suicide, I find that mostly, the line taken is much harsher.

Although I am by choice a non-practising Jew, I do find myself thinking about the issue in Jewish terms (I have been reading Gershom Scholem on *tikkun* today, for example) and I wondered if you knew of any texts in English that might help me to think this through.

I must admit that both my brother and I had difficulties with our religious background, but I still associate it with home and family – often I find that the less Jewish my life gets, the more Jewish my writing gets. It needs to find expression somewhere.

Anyway, thank you for reading this, and – again assuming I have the right person – for your kind words five years ago.

With best wishes,

Joanne

So I had asked my question, and the rabbi answered:

Hi, Joanne,

It is so meaningful to hear from you. I find it pretty amazing that you write to me today, as just yesterday as I was searching for something in my database I came across your brother's name. Although the time has passed, I still so vividly recall meeting both you and your mother and I am sure that the pain never fades or truly goes away.

I am sorry to hear of your mother's passing. I have no doubt that your presence in her life, especially in recent years, brought her so much comfort. My heart goes out to you that you went through so much loss in such a short time span.

As for your question in regards to some Jewish texts on suicide and your comments on how you have been finding a more harsh line in your research:

There is no doubt that from the perspective of Jewish law and its writings, suicide is forbidden. The Torah states: 'However, your blood which belongs to your souls I (G–d) will demand'.[*] This includes one who takes his own life. Since our life doesn't belong to ourselves any more than

---

[*] Writing God's name in full is forbidden for Orthodox Jews.

anyone else's life belongs to you or me. All life belongs to the Giver of Life – and He doesn't appreciate life being destroyed wantonly.

Nevertheless, it important to understand and accept there are those who commit suicide out of extreme distress or emotional agony. Therefore it is entirely left up to the Knower of All Souls (same one as the Giver of Life, aka G–d) to know whether this person really had any free choice left in his soul. This is not something that any fellow human being can conclude on our own, as we do not truly know what was going on within that person at that specific time.

That is why Jewish law holds that as long as no one actually saw the person committing suicide, or as long as no one actually knew what was being expressed at that very moment, we assume that the person was under extreme distress or emotional agony, and was therefore not responsible for his/her actions.

The basis of the sentiments I shared with you and your mother at your time of mourning. You can find more insights on this topic, as well on the concept of death and mourning in Jewish writings here: [_____]

I find it fascinating that you write that 'the less Jewish my life gets, the more Jewish my writing gets'. There is an old Jewish saying that 'The Pen is the Language of the Soul'. I believe firmly that within every Jew, regardless of affiliation or level of religious observance, there is a soul which is alive and burning. At times it may express itself more in writing then in practice, but it is there nonetheless, in its full glory.

I appreciate your note as it is meaningful to see that a
conversation from so long ago can still linger on. Please be in
touch and let me know if I can help further in any way.

Best,

Rabbi _____

We emailed back and forth a couple more times. He asked if he
might see the poems I had already written about my brother's
death and I sent them to him. Then he suggested that the complex
questions I was bringing to him might be more fully addressed by
a rabbi closer to home, and offered to refer me to a colleague in
the town where I live. I hesitated: what I had said about having
'difficulties with my religious background' had been something of
an understatement – in the three years between my brother's death
and my mother's, there were times when I had experienced a real
physical revulsion at the prospect of any kind of religious practice –
but, as I had also said, there had been some comfort in making the
proper arrangements for my mother's funeral, so I agreed.

In the traditional Jewish tales, people bring their questions to
the rabbi in his home. I met this second rabbi in coffee shop. What
I saw was what I had expected to see: full beard, no offering of
his hand to a woman, black coffee in a paper cup from this non-
kosher place. One of *them*, in other words – but then he spoke,
and I recognized the voice immediately – a young Jewish man
from north London, with an accent exactly like my own – that
is to say, one of *us*. I was still glad that I had decided not to buy

my Christmas wrapping paper before I met him that morning: I hadn't wanted to seem aggressive.

He got his black coffee in a paper cup, I got my tea with milk in the house crockery and we found a table together upstairs. I explained what had brought me there: my brother's suicide, the difficulties in the family, the pressure we had both felt to practise, the tension it had caused when first one of my male cousins and then my brother married out and had non-Jewish children, while my own marrying out had not seemed to bother anyone much. Jewishness, I should remind the reader, is passed down the maternal line: that way, it matters less who rapes us.

'And you feel you had an easier ride because of that?' the rabbi asked.

'Exactly,' I said.

The rabbi made an irritable noise. 'That Jewish continuity thing,' he said. 'It really gets to me. I don't think continuity by itself is a good reason for doing anything.'

I had not been expecting that: to hear him say something that could have come from my own mouth. I relaxed a little.

'Neither do I – nothing was ever explained to us growing up. You do what you do because we've always done it. They never explained why in Hebrew classes – they just assumed we would—'

'Don't get me started on Jewish education…'

'I don't think either of my parents actually believed in God – I know my dad certainly didn't – they practised to carry on the tradition, but my brother never saw what the point was if you didn't believe in it, and to be honest, neither do I.'

'Mainstream Judaism: it's like the Church of England.'

'It is: you don't pay attention in *shul*,* you sit and whisper and fidget, and all the older kids try and get out before the sermon. You're just there because you're there, and no one gives you a reason.'

'I hated it too – I wanted more rigour – that's why I went to the seminary instead of sixth form.'

'What did your parents think?'

'They weren't happy.'

'But they said yes?'

'No, but I went anyway.'

Out-rebelled by a rabbi. I told him what I had told his colleague, that the less Jewish my life, the more Jewish my writing.

'I've been reading about Kabbalah,'† I said.

'Oh yes?'

And so I started talking about the creation story, the story of the world as I understood it so far. Before the beginning, there was only *Ein-Sof*, the No-End, the Infinite, God existing in perfect, timeless completeness, with neither room nor need for anything other. But it came about that *Ein-Sof* decided to create the universe, and for this he would need to leave space, so he entered into himself, contracted himself into a hand's breadth, an act known as *zimzum*.

---

*   Synagogue.

†   Jewish mysticism.

In this way he created a vacancy, an area of darkness in the world, into which part of his substance emanated, bringing into being a primordial universe of pure spirit, divine light.

Within *Ein-Sof,* there is neither separation nor differentiation, neither subject nor object, neither darkness nor light, neither mercy nor judgement, but in the process of contraction and emanation, there was a separating out of the different aspects of the divine, the Ten *Sefirot.*

For one beautiful instant, everything was in its proper place, but then the catastrophe happened. For each *Sefirah*, a vessel was created. Finite and imperfect as they were, however, these vessels were unable to contain the godly essence even in its separate parts – almost immediately, they shattered. A new universe came into being: disordered, material, temporal, and containing, for the first time, the possibility of evil. The fragments of the first vessels, the *kelippot,* were scattered through the universe, sparks of divine light now trapped in the fallen, material world.

The counterpart of this primordial break, in the history of all peoples, is the expulsion from Eden; in the history of the Jewish people, it is the destruction of the First and Second Temples and the Exile from Zion. For Jews, every subsequent loss is an echo of this one, the founding loss: when we sit shiva at home for our dead relatives, and the synagogue officers come with the prayer books and the low-slung plastic mourners' chairs, they always bring along a little card that says, 'May God comfort you among the mourners for Zion and Jerusalem.'

⁂

The First Temple was destroyed by the Babylonians in 586 BCE*
and its replacement, the Second Temple, by the Romans in 70
CE. Both catastrophes are commemorated once a year, in high
summer, on the Jewish date of Tish'ah b'av, the 9th of Av. On this
day, the Book of Lamentations is recited publicly in synagogue,
with other laments, commemorating other disasters, added into
the liturgy.

In Lamentations, the sacked city of Jerusalem is personified
as a woman, bereft and humiliated, grieving for her many losses.
As I lived through the deaths of my brother and mother, the
clearing out and sale of our family home, and then the second
clearing out and sale of my mother's flat, which represented my
last secure foothold in the city of my birth, I was haunted by the
lines that open the first Book of Lamentations, the first lines of
the King James version:

'How doth the city sit solitary, that was full of people!'

Poor, wretched Daughter of Zion, ripped from her home,
her people, her context; she must now 'dwelleth among the
heathen'. Of course, the Daughter of Lamentations has been
taken into captivity, whereas I undoubtedly chose to dwell
among the heathen, but I never thought, when I made that
choice, that my old home and the nuclear family who lived in

---

* 'BCE' stands for 'Before the Common Era', an acceptable alternative
for the more specific 'Before Christ'. We also have 'CE' instead of 'Anno
Domini'.

it would be so comprehensively lost. That I would sit solitary, dwelling among the heathen, scrabbling for a home in the margins of an ancient text.

**

There's before and there's after: before and after the breaking of the vessels, before and after the Exile, before and after my brother's suicide. I explained to the rabbi that his death was the point of fracture in my world.

'When he did that,' I said, 'it sent out cracks in all directions – all the way through the family story, past and future. Everything I think I remember, I have to question now. I don't know where the problem started – it's all fragments. And it's up to me to gather them because I'm the one that's left.'

Gathering fragments: it's the task for which Jews have been chosen – assuming we've been chosen for anything – and if the primordial fragmentation was the cause of our Exile and dispersal through the nations, then the repair is its purpose. We must find the sparks of divine light trapped in the world and release them so that everything can return to wholeness and harmony. And so that the Messiah can come. For the first time, obviously. (What, you think he's been here already? Really?)

This work of gathering and repair is called *tikkun olam*, the 'repair of the world'. Orthodox Jews believe they can accomplish this through prayer and meditation, through observing *halakhah* – the Jewish laws – and through good works.

'I have always liked the idea of *tikkun olam*,' I said, 'but I have a secular version – it's about good works, trying to make the world better, trying to mend things.'

'That's not such a bad way to see it.'

'Even when it doesn't seem to make any difference, I believe we have to try.'

'Are you familiar with *Pirkei Avot* at all?'

'*Pirkei Avot*? No, I've only seen the words – I don't know what they mean. I never retained any Hebrew.'

'*Pirkei Avot* are the Sayings of the Fathers. I was thinking in particular of what Rabbi Tarfon said: "It is not for you to complete the work, but you are not free to idle from it."'

'So we won't achieve perfection, but that's no excuse not to try?'

'Exactly.'

'I like that.'

'So do I.'

The rabbi told me he was planning to run a study group on *Pirkei Avot*. He thought I would find it very rewarding – would I think about it? I said I would. Our drinks were finished, the conversation at an end. We said our goodbyes outside the café, then he went off to wherever his work was, and I went home to mine.

Vessel One

Q: What is the traditional response on first hearing of a death?

A: *'Blessed be God, the true judge.' This is the short form of the blessing, which is used for the news of any death, regardless of one's relationship to the deceased. When a Jew is one of the chief mourners, he should recite the blessing in its entirety: 'Blessed are You, Lrd our Gd, King of the Universe, the True Judge.'*

⁑

It's 15 August 2008, the middle of the summer holidays. Chris, my husband, is at work; our five-year-old son is at a holiday club; I am alone at home, supposedly writing but really just drifting about the house – I am too hot. The phone rings. It's my Uncle Richard.

'Joanne? It's Richard. I've had some awful news from America – some really terrible news. I think you'd better sit down.'

'What is it?'

'Julian committed suicide last night.'

'Oh God – how? What happened?'

'I don't know. Someone from his lab found our number – no idea how – and phoned.'

'Does Mum know yet?'

'No – we're going to drive down and tell her. Don't phone her yourself. I think it's best she has someone with her when she hears the news.'

That makes sense. I agree not to phone Mum, but not long afterwards, before her brother has reached her and before my husband has reached me, she phones for a chat and knows at once from my voice that something terrible has happened, and then I'm forced to tell her myself. The first thing she says is that she feared this might happen; the second is that she has to book us some plane tickets.

∗∗

Here is the first scene in the story of me and my brother: I see my grandmother carrying a blanketed bundle along the long, long aisle of a toyshop so vast that from my vantage point, I can't even imagine where the walls might be. She keeps going along the aisle, putting one foot in front of another, and suddenly a baby arm shoots out of the blanket and points at a Tiny Tears doll. She asks the bundled baby a question, something like, 'Is that what you want for your sister?' and takes it off the shelf.

I was always told that Tiny Tears was the present my brother gave me when he was born. I think by the time I was old enough to ask who gave it to me, I must have realized that my grandmother was a far more likely benefactor, but I also knew that my parents would never lie to me about something so important, so to stop the two stories from arguing, I imagined a new story: about my brother, my grandmother and the impossibly big toyshop. And I still say that the story of the toyshop is my first true memory of my life as a sister.

*

There are tooth marks on my passport. I put it in my mouth while Mum and I were queuing to check in and the resistance it offered felt like an invitation to bite, so I did. Now that we're on the plane, my passport is tucked away in my bag, so I've had to bite down on the ball of my thumb instead.

We are sitting in the back row of Economy on a plane bound for Chicago, where we will change for our internal flight. I have flown to the States a few times before, but always to New York – JFK or Newark. On the New York planes you are never more than two rows away from someone ordering kosher. But this is a plane to Chicago, and the two gangly boys in the seats in front of us are Mormons, on their way home from a mission.

I once opened the door of my parents' house to a similar pair of smiling young men. When I told them we were Jewish, they asked which tribe. I know they are fond of converting us posthumously. I expect they'll already have harvested my dad, my aunt and all my grandparents; they'll be gleaning my brother soon.

But I feel mean, thinking like this. All I really have against the boy in front of me is that he is reclining into my space, and that he is entitled to do.

Mum is on my left, in the window seat, with her eyes closed and her iPod on. I always take the aisle seat when I can: that way I won't panic every time the plane banks, making the window fill with Earth or Space, Death or the Infinite. Which would be worse? My brother used to talk about it sometimes. He was sure that death was the end, and it didn't scare him. It was irrational, he said, to be afraid of something you wouldn't be there to experience.

I am irrational. I am terrified of death. I am terrified of flying; had I not been, I might have visited my brother. If I had seen him, I might have realized how desperate he was; I might have prevented this.

I bite my knuckles, for a change. It's very painful. *Good.*

*

Which tribe are you from? In the biblical sense that the Mormon at my door intended, the answer could only be Benjamin or Judah, as the other ten tribes were lost after the biblical Israel split into two kingdoms and the more northerly of these was absorbed into the Assyrian empire. Whether I am literally descended from one of the sons of Jacob is debatable: Judaism was once a proselytising religion, after all. If I wanted to see my Jewish identity in tribal terms, then I would have to widen the definition of my tribe to encompass all other Jews.

Sometimes I do find it useful to think of Jewish society as tribal – not ethnically tribal, whatever that might mean, but *anthropologically*. All the aspects of my upbringing that strike my husband as alien – the importance of kinship and genealogy, the adherence to ritual and tradition, the life centred round a small community in which everyone knows everyone else – have a flavour of the pre-industrial about them. Traditional societies are a bit like human pyramids: no one member can move too far without threatening the integrity of the entire structure. In 'And the One Doesn't Stir Without the Other',* Luce Irigaray describes how the identities of mother and daughter are intertwined – fused, even. Imagine that concept extended, so that the daughter does not stir without her mother, her father, her brother, her aunts, her uncles, her cousins, her grandparents, her great-uncles, her great-aunts and her first cousins once removed.

As Nancy K. Miller, the Jewish American critic, puts it: 'How do you remember your life? How can you even tell it's your life, and not that of your tribe?'†

*
*

My last real conversation with my brother – which may as well stand for so many similar ones – took place one Sunday afternoon,

---

* Luce Irigaray and Helene Vivienne Wenzel, 'And the One Doesn't Stir Without the Other', *Signs*, 7.1 (Autumn 1981), pp. 60–67.

† Nancy K. Miller, '"But enough about me, what do you think of my memoir?"', *Yale Journal of Criticism*, 13.2 (Fall 2000), pp. 421–436, p. 423.

a few months before he died. He phoned me to talk about his best friend.

'You know Elliott's having his transplant soon?'

'Is he? In the hospital here? Down the road?'

'Yes.'

'So that's stomach, both parts of the small bowel, pancreas…'

'… and they're "throwing in a spleen", he said… They've only ever done it on a few people.'

'I know – you said. You must be so worried.'

'Worse than worried. You know there's always the danger of rejection – he might not come through. If the worst comes to the worst, it might be the last chance I ever get to see him, so…'

He took a deep breath. I interrupted:

'Of course you can stay here!'

Julian carried on as if I had not spoken, as if he were reeling off something he'd memorized and was scared of losing his place.

'… I'd like to come and stay with you, but this is the thing – I don't want you to tell Mum I'm in the country.'

'What?'

'I can't come unless Mum doesn't know.'

'But why not? I know you've not been getting on but—'

Julian reeled off his side of a story I already knew too well, the one about Mum's latest disastrous visit to the States. Julian had paid for her plane ticket to California, where he and his wife were attending a conference, so that Mum could look after their toddler daughter Giselle. Her last few visits had ended with the two of them barely speaking, but they both hoped that this time it would work out better: Mum was pleased that Julian had asked her for help, that he had paid for the trip; he was delighted that she had agreed to come. But then:

'Mum neglected Giselle – she left her strapped into her stroller all day, in her dirty diaper all day, so Giselle got this terrible rash and her clothes were ruined. And Mum kept complaining she was bored, and there was nowhere to go – we told her before she came over what it would be like, we thought she came because she wanted to help, but then she expected us to entertain her. And then the worst thing was, when we were in the last plenary session, I suddenly heard 'Daddy! Daddy!' and she was standing in the doorway of the conference hall holding Giselle, and when Giselle saw me she cried, and they had to stop the speech while I went to her – in front of everyone, it was horrible…'

'Mum said Giselle cried every time she tried to take her out of the buggy – she said she gave up in the end.'

'I know what Mum said, but the fact is she neglected Giselle.'

'She didn't mean to!'

'She doesn't care about her. She's constantly comparing her to your kid, as if he were the standard.'

'Mum compares everyone to everyone – it's a tick she's got.'

'Well, we think she's rejected Giselle, and we think she's rejected her because she's not Jewish, and she's half Japanese.'

'Mum's not a racist.'

'Do you know what the first thing she said was when I showed her Giselle? The very first thing?'

'No.'

'It was "Ooh, she's very dark, isn't she?"'

'Oh dear... but she won't have meant anything by it... She thinks Giselle's gorgeous – she tells everyone that.'

'But she's always saying stuff like that when she comes here. She commented on the food we had in the fridge – she said it was all Japanese stuff, there was nothing for her to eat there. And we had to get a separate fridge for when she comes, so that we can move our usual food to the basement and fill the kitchen fridge with stuff just for her – because otherwise she'll just keep going on about it.'

'But you know what Mum's like – she always says the first thing that comes into her head. She doesn't mean anything by it, she just doesn't think.'

'But she says things – things with needles in – and they just kill me, Joanne, they just *kill* me. Maybe she's different with you.'

'No, I don't think she is. And actually she's always said things to me – and not just recently. Always.'

'Really?'

'Yes. Always.'

'Like what?'

So then it was my turn to tell a story about Mum, the one about when I was twelve years old and my period started on a Saturday night while Mum and Dad were out and we were at home with the babysitter. I understood what had happened – because whatever else you might say about Mum, at least she prepared me for that – so I went to our parents' wardrobe where I knew she was keeping the sanitary towels for me, and I sorted myself out. Then later, when she came home, I told her my period started and she said:

'"Are you sure? Are you sure you weren't just *fiddling down there?*"'

'*Jesus!*'

'Oh come on – it's quite funny, really, isn't it?'

'I don't think so. I think it's terrible. I'm sorry you're stuck with her in the UK, I'm sorry you have to deal with her by yourself. She's got mental health problems – don't you think she should have some sort of counselling?'

'She wouldn't accept it. Look, I know she's difficult, but I don't think she realizes what she's doing when she says those things – I think that's why she doesn't remember them. I confronted her about the period thing once, and she just said I had fantasies about her. You'll never get her to see what she's done wrong. She's too old to change.'

'I suppose so.'

There was a long transatlantic pause, filled with despair.

'Look,' I said, 'why don't you come over, and we can have one meal with Mum, just one, and I'll be there, I'll make sure it's all OK, I'll be a buffer—'

'But no! I can't see her! I can't do it! She'll say something, and it'll just kill me!'

'But I can't do what you're asking me – it's too much, and anyway, even if Chris and I could keep our mouths shut about you being here, you can't expect our boy to.'

'Oh. No, I hadn't thought of that.'

All the life had gone out of his voice.

'OK, just leave it, then.'

'But you should see Elliott – don't let it stop you seeing Elliott—'

'No, no, it can't be helped. Just leave it.'

I thought we had, but an hour later he phoned me again.

'I've been thinking about what Mum said to you, and I've realized it makes me really *angry* – I mean, no wonder you're so fucked up!'

'But I'm not fucked up – OK, maybe I used to be, but I'm fine now.'

'No! You're *not* fine, you're *not* fine – you've always been completely messed up and it's because of Mum!'

'But I've found a way to deal with her—'

'No, no, you haven't – you're just protecting yourself because you have to deal with her every day. Our therapist says we were emotionally abused.'

'No! Mum wasn't perfect, but she meant well, she really did.'

Across the sea, my brother sighed. I tried to explain myself.

'But, Julian, we're both parents ourselves now. What I've realized is, it's not what you mean to do that has the bad effect on your kids – it's the things you can't help doing… Can't you please come over? Don't not come over because of this...'

'I just don't feel I'm getting anything out of the relationship with Mum any more.'

That stopped me in my tracks – it had never occurred to me that it might be possible to break up with one's mother. And then I said the thing – the thing with needles in – that of all things I would give years of my life to unsay:

'Except £20,000.'

I heard my brother's sharp intake of breath, as if he were in sudden pain ('it just kills me'), and with that the thread between us – that had held so long, at such a great distance – snapped beyond repair.

∗∗

Having arrived where we do not belong, Mum and I must join the longer queue at immigration. We spend the next hour and forty-five minutes slowly shuffling forward, while a piped voice welcomes us to the United States at five-minute intervals, and reminds us to keep queuing. Department of Agriculture beagles move in and out with their handlers, sniffing for contraband. We shuffle round a corner. The people in front of us tell us all about their trip, and we avoid telling them about ours. We shuffle towards the next corner, and check our passports again. At the far right, at the end of the row of immigration desks, people without passports sit in a cage – they are in full view, a warning. I wonder what I would have to say to get deported straight away, to be excused all this. 'Fuck you and fuck America!' – how about that? How about I shit in my hand and throw it at them?

No. That's not me, it never will be. When we reach the desk, the officer apologizes for the wait. He is a human being. He has a very sweet voice, and his toffee-brown eyes match his hair.

'What's the reason for your visit, please?'

Mum starts crying. I lean towards the officer over the desk, and we have the conversation that will serve as a template for so many others.

'Family business. My brother's just died. He lived in Plainsville.'

'I'm sorry for your loss. He must have been young. Was it an accident, may I ask?'

'No, there wasn't an accident.'

'Was he ill?'

'In… in a manner of speaking… I suppose he must have… He took his own life.'

'Oh, I'm sorry to hear that.' The officer taps a few computer keys. 'Could you look up into this camera, please? Thank you. Was he married? Did he have any children?'

'Yes, he was, and yes, he did.'

At this, with quite exquisite sadness, the officer shakes his head.

'That's so sad… I just don't understand it… I just don't understand why someone with a family would do something like that. I'm so sorry. Could you place your forefinger and thumb on here for me, please? Thank you… Well, I have to say, if that's

OK... in a way I know what you're going through... I lost my own brother a few years back.'

'I'm sorry,' I say in my turn, as he returns my passport. He then asks my mother for hers, and as he takes her details, her irises, her fingers, he continues with his story.

'He didn't have a family, though. He was a junkie, had been for a long time. He went fishing on a lake, and then he went missing – drowned.'

'I'm sorry,' I say again. 'That's hard.'

We both shake our heads. Such a sweet, sad man, a voice like treacle. Perhaps I could send Mum on to fetch the luggage while he and I have mournful sex in a broom cupboard. But he gives my mother her passport back, and we say goodbye.

Chicago airport is the size of a city. We start with a long walk to baggage reclaim. From there, we take a bus to another terminal, and then we take another long walk to the departure gate, where we wait a long time.

First, the flight is delayed. When the plane arrives, they let us on almost straight away, but then it doesn't leave, and it doesn't leave, and it doesn't leave... One of the stewardesses keeps going up to the door and looking through, waiting for a signal, but it doesn't come. At last we are told there is a problem with the engine; someone will have to carry out checks before the plane can be confirmed safe to fly. A couple of men in overalls appear and bang about in the cockpit for a while; then the pilot comes out and stamps down the aisle. He looks furious.

We are going to be very, very late arriving. Mum is in a state again: she has convinced herself that my brother's wife will be meeting us or at least waiting up for us and that she will become even more distressed by our lateness. After forty-five minutes or so, I realize that she needs me to look as if I'm doing something, so I go up to the stewardess and ask if she can say how delayed we are going to be. She asks if we want to leave the plane. I say, no, no, no and then, to my shame, I start to cry.

'We don't want to leave, we have to stay, it's just that there's someone *very distressed* waiting for us at the other end – could we get a message to the airport? Can we do that?' I can't seem to stop talking; the whole story gushes out. The stewardess is a kind listener, but there is nothing any of us can do. A little later, when she comes round to distribute complimentary drinks, she pats my arm, like a nurse.

Eventually, we take off. We fly through the Midwestern night, over sleepy cities with their regular grids of sodium lights, over fields and water towers and long, long highways. The scale befuddles me. Mum is reading a medieval mystery; she is holding the present at arm's length, and who could possibly blame her?

⁎

It was a Saturday, not long after Mum's disastrous babysitting trip. She appeared at our front door at her usual time, loaded up with handbags, overnight bags, knitting bags and carrier bags full of food and books and newspapers. My son poked his head out of the living room to say hello to his grandma and see if she had any presents for him. She distributed her bags in little heaps through the living room and dining room, then followed me into the kitchen where I was putting the kettle on. She said what she always said after she'd said hello.

'Haven't heard from your brother…'

'Oh.'

'Have you?'

'No. Not since the last time.'

'No email?'

'No. I did mention the money the last time I wrote, but I haven't heard back – about that or anything else. I think he's swamped at work at the moment.'

Mum pressed her lips together and leaned on the worktop.

'I really thought he'd repay it, once the money from the house came through.'

My brother, my cousins and I had just sold a house we had inherited together and Julian had been going to pay our mother her money back out of his share.

'I know. I don't know why he hasn't – like I said, I think he's just swamped.'

'But still… you know, my financial adviser didn't want me to lend the money – he advised against it.'

'I know.'

'It's really eaten into my capital.'

'Yes, you said.'

'I think I'll just have to sell the house and move somewhere smaller.'

'Really? Do you really have to?'

I pictured the house in Stanmore where my brother and I had grown up, imagined it emptied, with Mum shutting the door for the last time, handing over the keys to another family. It was not as if I enjoyed visiting there much, but there were all the younger versions of myself and my brother still running around the rooms and the garden, and they would be left homeless.

'I was thinking about it anyway. It's too big for me now.'

'It's your house. It's up to you.'

I passed her a mug of tea. She gave the quick little sigh that meant she was going to start on my brother again.

'You know, he told me not to tell Ayako he was borrowing the money – he seemed to be in some kind of trouble. I can't help wondering if he might have a gambling addiction?'

'No idea.'

'Or maybe it's just he's been spending too much. You're the only one of us who's any good with money. Your father was terrible. Did I ever tell you he used to run up debts and hide the statements from me?'

'No, you didn't.'

'I used to get so angry. And now Julian… He was crying when he asked for the money, he said he was scared he was getting just like Dad.'

'Really? He didn't say anything to me… Poor Julian.'

'But I really thought he'd have given me back the money by now.'

'I know. You said.'

By now we had sat down at the dining-room table, out of earshot of my son. She was ready to have her first cry of the weekend, and return to the scene of the conference hotel.

'I don't know why he won't *speak* to me, Joanne! I don't know why he makes me out to be such an *ogre*!'

I found a tissue and passed it to her. She lifted her glasses, wiped her eyes and carried on.

'They were so angry with me because I left Giselle in the buggy. But she screamed every time I took her out – I didn't know what else to do… And when I turned up at the door with her, it was the same thing, I didn't know what to do. They just left her with me, and she didn't know who I was, she wanted her mummy and daddy!'

'I know.'

'… and I tried to explain at breakfast the next morning, but he just brushed me off. He did give me a hug at the airport and said thank you for looking after Giselle, but when I got home he'd sent me the most awful email…'

'I know. I'm sorry. I wish I knew what to say.'

But I could never say anything.

∗∗

It's past one in the morning, and we've finally landed in the middle of the middle of America. We have no idea who to look for, but the moment we arrive on the concourse, a pair of young women approach.

'Hi! You're Julian's sister, right?'

'Yes, I am. It's really obvious, isn't it?'

My strong resemblance to my brother, the absurdity of it, with the nine-inch height difference and the opposite genders, has always been a standing joke between the two of us, and everyone who knows us both. Being the girl, I always suspected the joke was mostly on me. Still, it's a good joke; it's broken the ice already. The young women introduce themselves as Erin and Becky, postgraduate students from my brother's lab. I introduce our mother and they apologize for our loss. I apologize back. I will keep doing this.

'So Julian was the older one?' they ask, as we head towards the car park.

'No,' I say, 'the other way round: I'm the big sister.'

'*Really?*' They sound genuinely surprised, and I wonder what happened to my brother's face since I saw him last.

To his version of our face – I mean, of the shared family face. I look like my mother too. She has taken over the conversation. I am glad to be able to step back. I hear her saying the phrases I've already heard, and will hear again and again: 'He must have been in such pain... If he were here, I could throttle him... I knew something was wrong, the last few months I've been googling him to see if he was OK...'

I tune out, as I've already learned to do, and try to take note of our surroundings, but there is little to see at this time in the morning. We are walking through a multi-storey airport car park, and car parks look the same everywhere. Becky's car is the only one left on this level – another reminder of how late it is.

Mum and I both get into the back. As Becky drives off, I notice the Christian fish symbol dangling under her dashboard. It makes me uneasy. Mum immediately gets her smartphone out and starts kvetching about the lack of a signal. There could be messages from home. Where's the signal? Shouldn't there be a signal by now?

'Maybe there *should*, but there *isn't* – just leave it,' I snap. The students exchange anxious glances, and I immediately feel ashamed; they don't know us at all and they're meeting us at our worst. I get my own phone out and look.

'There you are – a signal. Do you have it too?'

She does.

'But there's no need to worry, is there?' I ask. 'The family know we're here, they can't be expecting to hear anything.'

'I want to let people know we've landed safely. Has anyone phoned ahead to the house? Does Ayako know we've arrived?'

'Ayako's been given something to help her sleep. You'll see her in the morning.'

'Oh, no, I don't want to *disturb* her,' Mum says. 'I feel so bad for Ayako – I can't believe what he's done to her…' I tune out again.

The fish symbol sways to and fro; we glide along the darkened highway. Mum asks if there are any plans for the funeral yet. More anxious glances: apparently my brother's already been cremated. There won't be a funeral, as such.

One day, a friend who has family in the States will explain to me that it is a common practice to cremate the body with no one present, then hold a memorial service later, but I don't understand this yet. Neither does my mother, and it strikes us both as irregular – incomprehensible, even – and we feel hurt, though no hurt was intended.

What I do remember is that a colleague of my brother's, who has been coordinating everything, spoke to my mother and asked if we wanted Julian to be embalmed. Mum said no, because it's not the custom for Jews to view their loved ones' dead bodies, and because the thought of seeing her son dead appalled her; I said no because I thought that embalming meant turning my brother into some kind of painted, stuffed dummy, and I might want to see him, but only as himself. Neither of us realized that it meant this, that we would arrive to be told he was already dust. We thought we were coming for a funeral; it never occurred to either of us that a family death could happen without one.

My brother's house is at the edge of town, in a new residential development, where there are big plots and no pavements. Even at this time of night, I can see that the front yard is full of beautiful flowers, and there are more in pots and hanging baskets round the door. I remark on this and Erin tells me what a keen gardener

Julian was. I didn't know that about him. Becky explains that this is a house where you leave your shoes outside. I didn't know that either. I leave mine next to a pair of men's lace-ups – my brother's shoes.

We step into a house of uneasy quiet, a house holding its breath between sobs. My brother's colleague, Lindsey, comes out into the hall to meet us and tell us that Ayako and Giselle are both sleeping now. My niece is in with her mother, so I am sent upstairs to spend what's left of the night in her room. As I climb the stairs, I catch sight of Erin weeping on Becky's shoulder. Sorry, so sorry.

When I switch the light on in Giselle's room, I see enough toys and books for a day nursery. My brother could shop like there was no tomorrow.

**

'What I'm hearing from you today,' my therapist said, 'is one long scream.'

We were sitting in the comfortable wooden outhouse she used as a consulting room, talking, as usual, about my mother, my brother and me. It was a few months before his death. Outside were the gentle garden noises, the running water and birdsong; inside the room there were neither demands nor interruptions. In twenty minutes or so I would have to leave and walk back to the station – that was the only hateful thing.

'I had a dream this week that I meant to tell you about.'

'Go on.'

'There were the three of us – Mum, Julian and me. We were at an antiques fair. Our parents used to take us to them quite a lot – I started collecting postcards and Julian collected cigarette cards, and—'

'Was this in the dream?'

'The collecting? No, sorry—'

'No need to say sorry.'

'So: the dream. We were at the antiques fair. Julian and I were walking around together, looking at things, talking – we were doing our own thing – then we turned a corner and suddenly Mum came charging up to us. She had her hands full of this big tangled heap of costume jewellery, and she just flung it into our hands, half and half, without asking, and said, "I need you to take care of the family hoard – I'm going to go round and get the car now, you can meet me at the back."

'And that was that – the trip was over, our hands were full and we had to go. I was grumbling about it while we were waiting and my brother just said, "You know she's always like this." And then she brought the car round and I woke up.'

'What was it you said she gave you? "A big tangled heap?"'

'Yes, it made me think about what you've said before, that the three of us are all tangled up together, not separated properly – a big tangled heap.'

'So you're all enmeshed.'

'Yes.'

'And now your brother's trying – in his clumsy way, perhaps, but he's trying – to get less enmeshed.'

I thought about this for a moment. I uncrossed my legs, then I wriggled my shoulders as if I were shrugging off a coat.

'He needs space – from Mum. From me too, for all I know. Well, good luck to him.'

⁎

As I write about my brother's attempts to get away, to untangle himself, I recall a poem I wrote in 1996. At the time I was trying to find my own space, and had moved up to Edinburgh, a city which my paternal grandmother complained would be 'too far away' for me and also 'very cold'. I was staying in a flat on Royal Park Terrace. It had a wonderful view of Holyrood Park, where flocks of Canada geese would stop to refuel after their long migration. I liked to watch them through my second-floor window as I tried to work. There was something about the way they waddled and fed in unison that I found both touching and familiar.

My Family Fly South

My family take off together,
flying south like a feathered arrow
pointing the way so that nobody
should forget.

My family believe in flocking together:
we're so alike we use each other
as mirrors, and for a crystal ball
I use my mother.

Pecking in the fields together,
my family squabble for corn and attention,
bringing every meal to an end
with a good row.

My family stick together
if attacked by outsiders. Setting our beaks
towards them, we flap our wings and launch
a united squawk.

My family plot a course together:
nothing else makes sense. We shout
after children who try to leave: You won't
get far on your own!

*
**

The first time I met my current GP was in the summer of 2002.
I remember how I sat down and burst into tears. A few weeks
before, I had miscarried my first baby at thirteen weeks. I had
chosen this doctor out of all the partners in the surgery because
she specialized in obstetrics and I thought that she would be

the best person to help me as I contemplated a fearful second pregnancy. I was right to choose so carefully.

Halfway through that pregnancy, my then-undiagnosed OCD flared up to the point where I was scared to cross roads, climb stairs or work in my loft office (in case of fire); before I would eat meat or chicken, I would examine the plateful, morsel by morsel, looking for undercooked bits, and every time I took a bite of anything, I was afraid that I would choke. The GP insisted that I take citalopram; I did and my crazy died down.

My son's birth was difficult. The GP came out to see us after we were discharged, admired the baby, admired the flowers in our living room and diagnosed an infected wound from my C-section. A few months later she diagnosed me with an underactive thyroid, and put me on the medication I'm still taking and will be taking for ever. Eighteen months later she confirmed my self-diagnosis of OCD and sent me to a psychiatrist. When I was too scared to go into town with my baby, she arranged for me to have a Home-Start volunteer and another from the local branch of Mind. Through all of this, she has always found the right help and nothing I've brought into her surgery has ever fazed her.

So it seems appropriate to bring her the news of my latest Adverse Life Event. A few weeks after my return from Plainsville, she is ushering me into her consulting room again.

'So what can I do for you today?' she asks. I'm not sure, but I tell her what's happened. Immediately she stiffens, moves almost imperceptibly back in her seat. I've made her uncomfortable. After all this time and all these disasters, I've actually made her uncomfortable.

'I'm so sorry. I can't imagine what that must be like.'

How many times I have I heard that already? A sentence so utterly respectful of the distance between my experience and the speaker's, and in its very acknowledgement of that distance, so utterly dismal to hear. As my GP utters it, I feel the walls of the room begin to extend and pull away from each other; by the time she has finished speaking, the surgery has become cavernous, and we have been stranded at opposite ends.

We talk a little longer. We agree that there's probably no point in increasing my medication. I'm already seeing a therapist so there's no point in her referring me to anyone else. There's nowhere else to take this.

'This is such a hard thing to live through,' she says. 'The hardest.'

She recommends a book; she can do that for me. And there's something else for me to take away, just a thought.

'It shows that you were right, at least – there is something up with your family.'

**

As the sole surviving child of that family, I find myself left with certain difficulties in the area of speech and language, problems of tense and person, and of definition.

To start with definition, does 'sole surviving child' effectively mean 'only child'? Now that I have no siblings, can I still define myself as a sister?

This leads into tense: unquestionably I *was* a sister, who *had* a brother, but if someone asks me, 'Do you [not did you ever] have any brothers and sisters?', how should I answer?

If I say, in the present tense, 'No, I don't,' am I declaring the truth, or concealing it?

And then – moving on to the question of person or persons – even if the sibling question has not explicitly been asked, when I tell, in the course of an ordinary conversation, an ordinary story about myself, do I talk about *my* parents, *my* childhood, *my* family, say that *I* grew up in London, *I* was brought up Jewish, *I* always went to my grandparents on a Saturday? Or do I say that *we* went the local school, loved to ride *our* bikes up and down the street, climbed trees on the wasteland that *we* called The Green and that, as *we* got older, *we* grew more and more impatient with *our* father?

My dilemma here is not that 'we' would be incorrect in the past tense, it is rather that – like the answer to the sibling question – the use of the first person plural has the potential to lead a casual conversation towards a revelation that would render it no longer casual.

So, Julian, what would you rather I did? Sprinkle a little bit of trauma wherever I go, or finish off what you started, and obliterate you? Which is your preferred legacy?

Vessel Two

Q: What is the Jewish attitude to death?

A: *Animals are entirely physical in nature, and angels entirely spiritual; the human being is unique in creation, being both physical and spiritual. In life, these two aspects of his nature exist in combination. At death, they separate: the physical part of his being – the body – returns to the dust, while the spiritual part – the soul, which is eternal – goes on to the next world.*

＊＊

I went to Hebrew classes every Sunday for six years, but I don't remember ever being told anything about this next world. When I asked my mother, she told me simply that the soul 'goes back to God'. She meant 'becomes part of God again' – dust to the dust, soul to the soul.

＊＊

Fitful, jet-lagged dozing. Every time I wake there is a little more light creeping under the window blind, and sleep is that little bit harder. Once I begin to hear voices, the distant thud of a fridge door, spoons clattering on bowls, I know I can't delay any longer. It's time to put some clothes on and face up to it.

The ground floor is open-plan, arranged around the stairwell. I follow the breakfast sounds for half a circuit, and find Lindsey and my sister-in-law standing by a small, round table at the back of the house, next to the kitchen. My niece is sitting at the table in her high chair. The two women are discussing how best to get her to eat.

'It was always so hard,' Ayako is saying. 'Julian used to feed her, but he couldn't get her to eat anything good, he would just give up, and I would come in and find them on the couch together in front of the TV, eating junk…'

'Never mind,' Lindsey says. 'For now, we just need to get something in her, anything, whatever she'll have.'

'Since Julian passed, all she'll eat are Goldfish crackers, and mac 'n' cheese…'

'Hi, Ayako.' She turns round, this woman I've only met once before, and we hug each other.

'I'm so sorry,' she says. 'I wasn't awake when you came last night.'

'That's OK,' I say. 'I know you needed to sleep.'

'Giselle, look, here's your Aunt Joanne – she's Daddy's sister.'

'Where's Daddy?'

Lindsey gives what is clearly a practised answer: 'Daddy's not here, Giselle. Daddy's dead. Daddy's in the sky.'

'Daddy's dead,' Giselle tells me.

'I know,' I say. 'We're all very, very sad, but it's so lovely to see you.'

And it is. She's a gorgeous, bright button of a child, I can see that already – but then I would: I'm her aunt.

Lindsey tells me and Ayako to sit down, and says she'll get me a cup of tea. Ayako starts to tell me what happened after she found my brother.

'The police were so horrible to me. They said it was a crime scene, they treated me like a suspect, they kept asking, "Why don't you have a copy of the letter? Why didn't he print it out?", like I must have written it myself. They were suspicious – I think they didn't like that I was foreign – and Giselle was in a state, and they kept saying can't you control this child, you need to put her upstairs, she's in the way...'

'Oh God,' is all I can say.

'I don't know that they were racist,' Lindsey says, 'but I do think you should complain.'

'I can't do that now.'

'Not now. Later, maybe. You could write something – get someone to help you with it.'

'Lindsey has been doing everything,' Ayako says, flatly.

'It's what you do,' says Lindsey, to me. Mum arrives. Ayako hugs her and apologizes again. Lindsey starts to lay out place mats, counting them out for Giselle.

'There's one for Mommy, one for Giselle, one for Grandma, that's three – and one for Aunt Joanne—'

'… and one for Daddy?'

'No, not for Daddy. Daddy's not hungry. Daddy's in the sky.'

'Daddy's dead.'

'That's right, Giselle.'

'I want Daddy.'

∗∗

Three months into her second pregnancy, my mother began to bleed. The flow became very heavy, and she was admitted to an antenatal ward. A junior doctor examined her, diagnosed an incomplete miscarriage and booked her in for surgery to remove what was left. My mother was left to reconcile herself to the loss of her child.

But that was not the end of the story. The consultant arrived at the foot of my mother's bed on his rounds, accompanied by the doctor who'd pronounced the child dead in the womb. The junior doctor relayed the patient's history to the consultant, explained the proposed treatment.

'And have you given this lady a pregnancy test?' the consultant asked.

No, he hadn't. And when he did, my brother was still there, alive. The bleeding stopped soon afterwards and my mother was discharged.

This was always talked about as a miraculous survival on my brother's part, evidence of a ferocious determination to be here in the world. He was induced two weeks early, after the placenta began to detach, but was born seemingly none the worse for it. After his circumcision, he was given the Hebrew name Chaim, which means 'life'.

⁂

Among the morbid and semi-mystical thoughts circulating in my head in the weeks and months after my brother's death, is the notion that he had been fated to die those thirty-six years earlier in the womb, and that by being saved at the last minute instead, by being born, and by living in the world for all those years, he had offended somehow against the preordained order of things, which had now, belatedly, reasserted itself. Maybe the time he had been living on was not borrowed so much as inadvertently stolen, like money accidentally deposited in one's bank account, which will be claimed back as soon as the bank realizes its error.

I've had these kinds of thoughts before, but not about my brother. My own son's birth was difficult; he had been trying to emerge from me at an oblique angle, and while he pushed on my cervix, and it failed to dilate, the placenta had begun to abrupt. A labour which had begun in the pool room just after lunch ended in theatre at two in the morning, with my son taken out by Caesarean section. While we were in the recovery room, the midwife told me that she'd overheard the obstetrician saying that they'd operated 'just in time'.

My son was a little ill after delivery, and during the five days we spent on the transitional care ward, that phrase, 'just in time', worked powerfully on my imagination. I supposed that we might both, in other circumstances – historical circumstances, Third World circumstances – have died horribly: I would have haemorrhaged to death, while my son suffocated. When I'd had a miscarriage before, I'd been encouraged by the doctors to see it as a successful instance of natural selection, and, if I followed that logic through, it could be said that what had happened when my son and I were saved was a case of natural selection interfered with. We weren't supposed to be alive; we weren't fit to be alive. That my thyroid failed soon after the birth, and that I was for ever afterwards dependent on artificial hormone replacement to survive just seemed to confirm that, in my case at least, it was a reasonable hypothesis.

**

The way our mother remembered it was that someone came to the front door, but as soon as they started speaking she and her older brother Richard were shoved into the front room and that door was shut behind them. Nobody sent them off to school that morning. Instead, our grandmother rushed out and when she came back, much later, it was to tell them that our grandfather had been hit by a bus and killed.

Our grandmother refused even to think about marrying again. She bought the burial plot next to her husband and went out to work. Our mother was sent to a children's home in High Wycombe, where they slept two to a bed and sometimes if her bedmate wet herself she might get hit on the bottom with a wooden spoon because no one would believe it wasn't her. She got an ear infection and screamed with the pain, but no one paid much attention until the drum burst, and she was always a little bit deaf after that. The other children in the home were jealous of her because she had a mother who visited sometimes and a home to go back to one day; they had all said goodbye to their parents in their own languages on railway platforms in other countries and had never seen them since.

Our mother really was more fortunate than the others: after two years our grandmother came to High Wycombe to take her home. They took a train back to London, then the Underground to Golders Green, and then a bus to Pennine Drive. It was not until they were walking up the little garden path that our grandmother decided to explain to my mother that the home she was going back to would be much more crowded than the one she remembered: our great-grandparents had been bombed out of their house in Lordship Lane, and now they were living in our mother's house, with more cousins, and more aunts.

Next morning, our grandmother went back to work. The aunts kept a close eye on our mother all day, looking for faults, and when our grandmother came through the door in the evening, tired and bad-tempered, they told her what they'd found. They did the same the next day. And the next. And then every other weekday for years and years and years.

⁂

Our mother went back to work herself, when we were small, but in calmer circumstances, and only part-time. At Edgware General Hospital, she was a medical social worker, and when she was at home she was our mother. She's there in the only very early memory of myself with Julian that I'm certain is a true recollection, rather than a story someone told about us. My mother is pushing us back from the shops at Honeypot Lane in our navy-blue pram with the big wheels. My brother is lying down in the main body of the pram while I am on the toddler seat fixed over the top, facing backwards. There is a white, lacy canopy over both of us, so it must be summer and my brother – who was born in May – must be very tiny indeed. We are just about to cross St Andrew's Drive, next to the big roundabout, and the leaves on the trees overhead are full and deep green, casting big shadows. I think Mum and I are both talking. I was always full of questions; my parents were fond of telling me that two weeks after my brother arrived, I asked, very calmly and politely, when he was going to leave.

.*.

We are in the middle of Tornado Alley here, so the house comes with a storm basement. To get down, all you have to do is open a door in the stairwell wall, just behind the breakfast table, and descend a short flight of stairs. I already know that this was the last door Julian passed through alive, and there is some small part of me that truly believes I might find him on the other side of it.

I ask Ayako if I might spend some time down there by myself, and she says of course, if that's what I need: it's not a crime scene any more, there's no tape and no taboo.

I have spent much of the journey here imagining this basement, and what my brother did to himself in it. Ayako told me the story herself over the phone, before I came over. She said they had only just returned home themselves, after spending a couple of weeks in Japan, where her parents still lived.

The flight had been long and tiring; they had been tetchy, the two of them, they had bickered. When they arrived back, Ayako went to bed to sleep off her jet lag. She was worried about Julian and suggested that he should sleep too, but he waved the idea away. He had things to do, he said; he was fine, would be fine. She was not to worry; she was to sleep.

My brother did the laundry. He went downtown, as he would have learned to call it, and bought groceries. A colleague at the chemistry faculty where my brother and his wife both worked ran into him outside the wholefood supermarket and had a brief conversation with him, the last Julian would ever have with anyone outside the house. At some point – maybe before that, maybe afterwards – my brother must have let himself into his lab, the one with his name on the door, and picked something up.

He dropped their daughter off at day care at the usual time and later, again at the usual time, he picked her up. Ayako said she must still have been asleep when they arrived. She had woken up a few times and heard Julian moving about the house, heard his voice and their little girl's. On one occasion – she wasn't sure when – he brought her a glass of water and they exchanged their last few words. He was fine, he said. He hadn't finished what he had to do. He didn't need to sleep, but she should.

Presumably, he did the usual things with and for his daughter: gave her supper, maybe watched a DVD with her, bathed her, put her in her pyjamas, read her a story. She had never been an easy child to get to sleep, and she was still a little distressed and disoriented from the jet lag. Perhaps that was why he left her sleeping on the couch and didn't take her upstairs.

He must have waited until he was sure she was safely asleep before he got on with the rest of his business. First of all he went online and made the financial arrangements, moving all his funds from his accounts into his wife's. After this was done, he opened up Word and wrote Ayako a note, saying that he didn't really know why he was doing what he was about to do, but that it seemed like the right thing, and that she and their daughter would be better off without him. Then, in much more detail, he explained what he'd done with their finances.

He didn't print the note out – perhaps he worried that the sound of the printer might wake their child up, or maybe it was that he only had enough energy and will left for a certain number of actions and no more, and to print and fetch a couple of sheets of paper would have taken him over the limit. But, that said, he did find it in him to fetch the whiteboard and pen, lay it on the table so that his wife would see it when she came downstairs, and write his final words:

LOOK AT THE

COMPUTER

Then he took the trash out. Judging by what was found in it afterwards, what he did next was to take the phial of potassium cyanide – that item he'd picked up from the lab – out of his pocket, drain the greater part of it and chuck the remainder into the trash. Then he stepped back inside, closed the door and went down the stairs to the storm basement, where he lay down on the old couch, folded his arms neatly over his chest, and ever so quietly died.

The first thing I notice is that the couch has gone, and whatever traces of my brother it held will have gone with it. I take a few steps into the centre of the main basement space, the den, where I know it must have been, and sit down on the floor. Bookshelves run along the walls on either side, and tell no coherent story. There are novels, English and American. I spot *Postcards* by Annie Proulx on the top shelf on the left; I never realized that we'd both read it, that it might have supplied some safe conversation material. There are other books he never mentioned – not novels, but the kind of books that are designed to uplift and improve, books to make him more assertive, books to make him less depressed, books that failed him dismally.

Then I catch sight of two very familiar books, hardbacks, one bound in burgundy and one in navy blue, and it jars me a little, as if I had travelled halfway round the world only to bump into a pair of elderly aunts. They are the Reform Synagogues of Great Britain prayer books, *Forms of Prayer*, the burgundy for 'Daily and Sabbath' and the navy for 'Days of Awe'. I have my own pair and, even though I don't believe, I would still kiss one if I dropped it on the floor. I could no more give them away than I could disown my family. Their presence here is a sign to me that, no matter what my brother said about Judaism or his upbringing or our mother, he could not really bring himself to let go. Or maybe it was just that he could not live with himself if he did.

I can't bear to stay with that thought. I look round the room for evidence of a more familiar Julian, the one I used to laugh with. It isn't hard to find. Straightaway I see the silly present I sent over with my mother on one of her visits, a two-volume set of the complete works of William McGonagall, the magnificently bad Scottish poet. Julian was always able to see the funny side of failure: his PhD thesis (*The Development of a Functional Model for Water Oxidation by the Oxygen-Evolving Complex of Photosystem II*) has the following epigraph, courtesy of W. C. Fields:

'If at first you don't succeed, try, try again. Then quit. There's no point in being a damn fool about it.'

Next to McGonagall is a hardback copy of *The Deeper Meaning of Liff*, a very useful dictionary compiled by Douglas Adams and John Lloyd, in which they match place names that don't mean anything to phenomena that have no names but really should do. When our father first brought the book home, Julian announced that he had found the perfect word for me in it: I was a 'greeley', a person who 'continually annoys you by continually apologizing for annoying you'. I laughed as much as he did, but Mum still told him off.

The far wall is taken up by a huge screen, part of the 'entertainment centre' left by the house's previous owners. The VHS cassettes piled up on either side are all of British comedy shows: *Blackadder* and *Red Dwarf*. Julian introduced me to *Red Dwarf* while he was still in the UK; after he moved to the US, he told me about *Seinfeld, The Animaniacs, Ren and Stimpy* and *Rocco's Modern Life*. I sometimes used to wonder if a sense of humour might be what we both had in place of a sense of proportion. My brother really couldn't afford to lose his. No joking.

**

I'm in my office in the loft, staring at the holdall with my brother's ashes in it, and talking to a friend on the phone. She's a Jungian analyst, so I don't feel I have to censor too much. I'm telling her how sick I felt on the flight back.

'And I *still* keep feeling nauseous – when I'm thinking about it all, but sometimes even when I'm not, I get these sudden waves of nausea. Sometimes I even retch.'

'OK... Do you mind telling me how your brother killed himself?'

'No. It was potassium cyanide. He got it from his lab.'

'And he ingested it?'

'Yes, he did.'

'Well, there you are then.'

*
*

My brother's house is filling up with people – *his* people: students, postdocs, colleagues. Becky and Erin are back, asking how we slept. Someone whose name I can't catch tells me I have cute clothes. Two of Julian's male students are inspecting the ride-along mower and trying to decide who'll get to cut the grass first.

There is a huge lawn at the back of the house – a big, flat square of the most extrovert green, divided from its neighbours by a low white fence. From time to time a rabbit or two will appear at the margins, confident that no one will chase them away. People mow lawns here but they don't walk on them, not in high summer anyway; the grass is full of 'chiggers', insect larvae that jump onto calves, burrow in and itch like fury. Since I've been warned about them, I only have to glance at the lawn to feel the need to scratch.

Chiggers underfoot, and overhead a merciless sun. The air in between is so densely humid that stepping out of the air-conditioned house feels like shoving my face into a warm, wet flannel. It's more hospitable inside. Neighbours in shorts and baggy T-shirts are dropping by with cakes and casseroles. People hug me, sometimes before they've even been introduced; I am so obviously Julian's sister that there's no need for anyone to tell them. Everyone has kind things to say about my brother.

'He was a great guy, we all really loved him.'

'Such a great supervisor, so supportive – I couldn't have done my work without him.'

'He was a brilliant chemist. I remember when he came to apply for the post, and he did his presentation, and I said afterwards, "We've *got* to have this guy!"'

'You know someone said to me, about him: "The stars that burn the brightest, burn out soonest."'

'He was really a bright star.'

'And he had this *great* sense of humour, he was so funny – do you remember that dinner, when he got drunk?'

'Yes! And he started going on about how bad Dick Van Dyke's British accent was in *Mary Poppins* – he said it was "a bloody disgrace" – and then he *did* Dick Van Dyke being British, right there at the table, at this formal dinner, he —'

'Was it like this, by any chance?' I ask. I ball my right fist up, then I pump my arm, screw one side of my face up and sing, 'It's a jawlee hawliday with Mea-ariee!'

The room erupts. 'Exactly! It was exactly like that!'

Then they look at me wistfully: 'You are *so* like him.'

Just before lunch, Lindsey takes me aside.

'I'm afraid the situation's got a bit complicated,' she says.

'OK.'

'Ayako can't cope with having your mother in the house.'

'Oh.'

'She says she's been talking a lot about the money Julian owed, and she just can't handle it right now.'

I had mentioned it first, because I knew that my mother would as soon as she had a chance to talk to Ayako.

'She doesn't mean to upset Ayako – she's in shock, like a wounded animal – she's just saying whatever comes into her head…'

'I know, I know. Ayako's the same – please don't be upset by her, she just has no filter at the moment…'

'She hasn't upset me… and I do understand why she might not want us here.'

'So can you talk to your mom?'

'Of course – I'll just say that it's too much for her having *us* to stay… so what do we do now? There are hotels?'

'Yes, don't worry, I'll phone round and get you some prices. Thank you. You seem like the rock of the family, so I knew I could be straight with you.'

So Julian was a star, I'm a rock and I've called my mother an animal. Events have propelled us beyond the human.

⁂

It's September 2011, and I am going to visit my mother in the Royal Free again. I got to know the place in 1997, when my grandparents died in it, and now it is becoming family to me all over again. The main building is still oppressively tall; the rising air still howls through its lift shafts. You can still admire the London skyline from its windows, but you will notice changes: the Crystal Palace mast, the BT Tower and Canary Wharf have been joined by the Gherkin and the London Eye. This time, Mum is in an oncology ward on the eleventh floor, and this far up, the vista is breathtaking.

Mum is in a four-bed ward, in the first bed on the left, sitting up, surrounded by books and washbags and sections of the Sunday newspaper.

'Did I tell you they drained the fluid off my lung? I'm coughing much less. I thought I might manage to walk down to the café?'

'Of course. Whenever you're ready.'

Mum gathers her things together. I take a look round the ward and think it might be the saddest one I've ever visited. The woman in the bed opposite is Belsen-thin; she is lying back with her eyes closed but I can tell she is not asleep – it is only that keeping her eyes open would require the kind of stamina she no longer has. The woman next to her, in the opposite corner, is sitting up with her laptop in front of her, her mother and children around her; although she is nowhere near as thin as her neighbour, her cheeks are hollow and her skin is yellowish-grey.

When Mum is ready we walk, very slowly, to the lift, past bays full of tiny, thin elderly men in striped pyjamas, all asleep with their mouths open. They look like the perfect definition of helplessness.

On the ground floor, if you take a right turn out of the lifts you come to the hospital shop and the ATM; take another right and there is a tiny branch of Costa Coffee, nicely positioned so that the patients at the outpatient pharmacy at least have something to drink while they're waiting. I order a cappuccino for me and a latte for Mum. When the drinks are ready, I carry them both to one of the sticky-tabled plastic booths.

'Dr Y. came to talk to me yesterday,' she said. 'I think, from what she said, that she was giving me a heads-up that they might pull the plug on the chemo…'

'And how would you feel about that?'

'To be honest, it's fine by me… Well, you know, the three treatments I've had have been absolute hell on wheels – I've ended up in hospital every time – and here I am again.'

'It's not been great, has it?'

'What do you think?'

'I'll say what I've said before, Mum – it's your choice. Don't carry on with the chemo for my sake. I mean… I don't mean I'm happy about the thought of you dying, I just mean… Oh, you know…'

'Thank you. I'm so fed up of people saying to me, "You're a fighter! You can beat this!" What a load of rubbish!'

'But the doctors never said it was curable.'

'I know!'

'I expect they say that because they love you, because they're scared.'

'I suppose so.'

'Mum, I think… I think when you've gone through what we've gone through with Julian, it puts some kind of iron in your soul. Most people don't have it.'

'Yes, I think you're right… A woman in her seventies dying of natural causes is hardly a tragedy. I've made my threescore and ten.'

She means it, and I know this because when we get back to the ward she reminds me once again that all her important contacts are on her phone, and that all the relevant papers are still where we filed them, together, just after she was diagnosed. The so tough-minded Limburg women, suffering no fools, facing facts.

Vessel Three

Q: If God is just, then how do we account for premature deaths, wasteful deaths, violent deaths and deaths which are preceded by terrible suffering?

A: *Certainly, when we look at our lives in this world, we see a great deal of undeserved suffering, but we need to remember that our perspective is limited, and that this world is not all there is; neither is this physical existence the be-all and end-all. God will make sure that justice is served in the long run. It is not for us to question His methods, or His reasoning: these are beyond our understanding.*

**

It hasn't been difficult to find us a hotel: there's plenty of space at the Best Western. I have a twin room to myself, with a view of the traffic going north and south on Delaware Street – though to my eyes it is less of a street and more of a motorway. Across from the hotel is a CVS – the Boots of America – and beyond that a stretch of empty-looking parkland. Next to the hotel on the left is a barn-sized Tex-Mex restaurant, and in front of that the intersection between Delaware Street and Lincoln Parkway, running west to east. The traffic lights at the intersection are hanging from wires over the centre of the road, and I think of *Twin Peaks*, of the lights changing red to green over the empty roads at night, while the town puts its dark secrets to bed and Agent Cooper dreams of Laura Palmer.

Real Middle America has no business looking so much like TV Middle America; it is as if Plainsville is not even *trying* to convince me that it is real, that my brother truly lived in such a place and truly died in it. A yellow school bus goes past, the first three-dimensional one I have ever seen: *The Simpsons*, I think, and *Charlie Brown*.

Arrangements have been made, for Ayako and for us. There is to be an informal reception at the house in a couple of days, and the faculty is going to hold a memorial service at the end of the week – they have brought it forward so that Mum and I can attend. Various kind people have volunteered to take turns to look after the two of us, to have us round to dinner, or show us round town. One of the faculty wives is to pick us up for breakfast tomorrow.

We are going to the Tex-Mex barn for dinner tonight, but that's hours away. I have already visited the computer in the lobby to check email and Facebook. I have a biography of William Blake with me (why?) but I can't read it. My iPod is charging. I'm tired but I can't sleep. I try making a cup of coffee with the strange little device in the room, but the powdered coffee creamer I have to use makes me gag after one sip, so I pour the rest down the sink. That leaves the television.

I think I'm bound to find a repeat of something familiar – *Friends* or *M*A*S*H** or even *Cagney and Lacey* – but all the channels I find seem to be showing either adverts for prescription drugs or news, and local news at that: from the town, or the state, or 'the Tri-State Area'. I find CNN but it isn't what I want; it isn't comfort viewing. Then I flip to something different, a piece of black-and-white entertainment from the 1950s, stretched uncomfortably over the twenty-first-century screen. A trio of wide-faced, smiling women with tightly moulded hair finish singing and are applauded, which makes them smile even more widely. Then a host in a tuxedo puts his hands together and introduces another man in a tuxedo, who is going to sing a solo. As the audience applauds again, the camera moves in until the whole screen is filled with his billowing face; his eyes ignite like a preacher's, and he sings of a bluebird of happiness.

∴

Prior to his move to Plainsville, my brother had lived first on the East and then on the West Coast, where there were plenty of other Jews: ultra-Orthodox, secular and all shades in between. Plainsville was quite different; although it was a university town, and where there are faculties, there are usually at least a few Jews, there was no doubt that as a couple – neither of them American, one of them Jewish, the other Japanese – they were different, and felt their difference, in a way that neither of them had before. This was, for the most part, nothing to do with any hostility from the people around them, who were welcoming, but nonetheless they were not American, they were not Midwestern, they weren't churchgoers of any kind.

They'd only really had one nasty moment. This was when they had visited a local covered antiques market and been horrified to come across a stall selling Nazi memorabilia. They had complained to the owner of the market, but he had been very unsympathetic; he rented space to whoever could afford it, he said, and what they chose to sell in that space was none of their concern. They left with a very unpleasant taste in the mouths, which lingered, to mingle with others, and never went back to the covered market again. I'm guessing that the Nazi memorabilia stayed where it was. I hope it never sold that well.

My brother identified with his Jewishness sufficiently to feel wounded by that stall and to complain about it, but he was not practising, nor did he believe. It took me longer to get to the same point, but I had, a few months before my brother died. I'd been declaring myself agnostic since my teens, and so I was, intellectually, but the full truth was more complicated. God slipped away from me by degrees.

The deaths, in one year, of our father, great-uncle, grandfather, aunt and grandmother might have cured me of any tendency to believe, but the opposite happened: through those months I had a very strong sense of God's presence. The repeated rituals of bereavement, with their commands to magnify and sanctify His name, had helped to do that, as had the sense that only some great power could sweep away so many in such a short time. This was the God of Job, of arbitrary, Old Testament wrath. So, at that point, I was very close to believing in Him – I just didn't like Him very much.

It was the miscarriage, five years later, that dislodged Him. The only way to make the event bearable was to drain it of any moral significance, to see it as impersonal. I took in what the doctors told me, repeatedly: that it was an 'independent event', that one in four pregnancies ended that way, that more pregnancies ended that way than we'd ever even realized. I thought about nature's tactic with reproduction, its tendency always to be so magnificently wasteful, to throw everything at the wall and see what stuck; all those thousands of fish eggs, spider eggs, insect larvae, destined to come to nothing, every one entirely dispensable. As long as the population reproduces itself, who cares about the surplus gametes squandered on the way? It was nature – blind, indifferent nature – and the lost baby and I were just a minuscule, animal part of it. It was chilling, but it helped me cope. How personally I took things was a function of how much I chose to see myself as a person, a being with a soul; without God to underwrite my personhood, neither I nor anything that happened to me had to matter. For the first time in my life, I felt I understood the consolations of atheism.

My mother wanted me to go with her to the Yom Kippur service a couple of months later, and I did, but I sat fuming, because if there was a God – and I really didn't think there was –

shouldn't *He* be apologizing to *me*? There's one line in the service that goes 'because we believe in spite of ourselves'. *Oh, bugger off and leave me alone*, I thought.

Externally, though, I allowed my Judaism to limp along for a while. I let my membership of the synagogue lapse, but kept saying, when Mum asked, that I was meaning to rejoin. At Passover, I went to seders* in other people's houses. I talked about teaching my son about his Jewish heritage.

For several years I hummed and hawed, evaded and prevaricated. When my son started school, there were three other Jewish children in his class, all of whom had two Jewish parents, and two of whom came from very Orthodox families. My son is a WASP-y looking child with a very English surname, so it would have been easy to have kept him away from them, but that seemed a craven approach to take, so I 'came out' to these other parents, and the most evangelical of them invited us, and my mother, around to Friday night dinner. We went a few times; my son found it all rather bewildering, but it mattered to me that he was Jewish, and it mattered to me that he should have some idea of what this meant – otherwise, as my father used to say, how will they know what it is they're rejecting later on?

In the spring of 2008, we went over for Purim. The basis of this festival, as of most Jewish festivals, is – as a friend's aunt put it: 'They tried to kill us; they failed; let's eat.' We have a religion

---

* A seder is a Passover service, held around the dinner table on either of the first two nights of the festival.

made of stories mostly, stories of us – and God – against the world. The central ritual in this festival is the communal reading of the story of Esther, the Jewish wife of the Assyrian king who saved her people from genocide by going on hunger strike. It's a raucous affair, with every mention of the chief villain, Haman, accompanied by loud, disrespectful noise from the audience. At the triumphant climax of the story he is hanged from the very gallows he has had built for the planned execution of his rival courtier, Esther's Uncle Mordechai. His plan to have the empire of Assyria ethnically cleansed of its Jews is foiled. He tried to kill us; he failed; let's eat our *hamentashan*, our pastry Haman's Ears.

This was as much of the story as I had known before that evening. But it went on, to show how the king reversed the edict against the Jews which Haman had persuaded him to issue:

> Letters were despatched by mounted couriers, riding steeds, used in the king's service, bred of the royal stud, to this effect: The king has permitted the Jews of every city to assemble and fight for their lives; if any people or province attacks them, they may destroy, massacre, and exterminate its armed force together with women and children, and plunder their possessions.

The note in the *Jewish Study Bible*, from which I've taken this passage, points out that 'Although distasteful to the modern

reader, this was normal in the ancient world.' At the moment that
I was reading those lines, I was suddenly sharply aware that I was
not in the ancient world, but alive in the modern one, where (like
Esther, come to think of it) I had married out of my people. And
at that moment, as I read about the reversal of Haman's edict, I
realized that it wasn't just the lack of belief in God that gnawed at
me, but the inescapable UsandThemness of the Jewish holidays,
the pressure I felt to identify first and foremost with Us when the
person I'd chosen to share my life with was one of Them (and
who has never shown the slightest desire, I should add, to convert
himself into an Us).* I became aware – fully, inescapably aware
– that when I tried to observe these holidays – Passover, Purim,
Chanukah – I felt torn in half, that I'd had enough of feeling torn,
and that, therefore, I'd have to face the consequences of truly
having had enough. That is to say, I'd have to tell my mother.

---

*   I feel bound to add here, in case it isn't crystal clear, that there is nothing
in Judaism that suggests that Jews should treat non-Jewish people with any
less consideration or kindness than they would treat other Jews. Leviticus
19: 17 says: 'Love your fellow as yourself: I am the Lord.' That's the *Jewish
Study Bible* version, though the King James Bible version may be more familiar to readers: 'Thou shalt love thy neighbour as thyself.' There are many
differences between the two translations, some extremely striking: the King
James version of the passage from Esther renders the line which ends 'if any
people or province attacks them, they may destroy, massacre, and extermi-
nate its armed force together with women and children, and plunder their
possessions' as 'Wherein the king granted the Jews which were in every city
to gather themselves together, and to stand for their life, to destroy, to slay
and to cause to perish, all the power of the people and province that would
assault them, both little ones and women, and to take the spoil of them for
prey'. What a great gulf in meaning there is, between 'plunder' and 'prey'.
I love the language of the King James, but I know full well it wasn't written
for me.

The difficulty of Telling My Mother – a difficulty cradle Catholics understand but many other non-Jews don't – is that a rejection of Judaism is not just the renunciation of a belief system, and of a certain set of habits, easily detachable, but also – unavoidably – of the way in which your family brought you up. Try doing that while protesting that you are not – honestly, *not* – actually rejecting your family, and then you might understand why so many Jews who practise – my father was one example – do so without any belief. They keep the Sabbath, up to a point; they marry other Jews and keep kosher homes with them; they have their sons circumcised and then bar mitzvahed, their daughters bat mitzvahed; they do their best to persuade their children to marry other Jews in their turn; they eat matzo over Passover; light candles for Chanukah; go to synagogue on the 'High Holy Days' of Succoth, Simchas Torah, Rosh Hashanah and Yom Kippur, and fast on the last day; they bury their dead in accordance with Jewish tradition, and when their time comes, they are buried alongside the others in the same manner. They do this, in many cases, not to keep a covenant with God, but to keep it with their mothers, fathers, aunts, uncles, grandparents, numerous dead from the Holocaust and pogroms and God-knows-what-else, because in doing all this they maintain their links with them, they affirm that they will not abandon their dead, they will not abandon each other; every practice, everything you do in the same way that your mother did is a little thread that ties you to her, and if you fail to maintain it, if you sever it or if it perishes from your neglect, that thread is lost; the memory of a culture that so many tried to destroy is gone, you've condemned them to oblivion.

So what do you mean, you don't want to practise any more?

When I told my mother that I wasn't going to rejoin the synagogue, that moreover I had realized that the kind of observance with which I had grown up was not for me or my family, her first question was, 'Then where will I go for Pesach?'* I don't remember the details of the rest of the conversation, only that it rapidly turned into a conversation about Julian, who of course wasn't talking to my mother at the time, and ended with her crying. A couple of days later I got a phone call from my cousin, to tell me how horrible it was to see my mother so upset. Surely I could do more to bring Julian round. If only I knew just how upset Mum was, I could do a bit more, couldn't I?

When I had explained my side of the story and put the phone down, I found myself shaking with anger. I called to mind all the times Mum had prompted me to try and persuade my brother to talk to her, to remind him that he owed her money. It would be a long time before I felt able to be that honest with her again; it felt like a failed experiment.

*
**

Mum had told me more than once that the reason she always kept a kosher home was that her family wouldn't eat there if she didn't. As kosher families go, we were stricter than some but not

---

*   Passover.

as strict as others: we kept separate cutlery and crockery for milk and meat, which my mother washed up in separate plastic basins; although we did not check the provenance of the meat we ate outside the home, we never ordered dishes with both meat and dairy in them; we never ate pork or shellfish. It still seems strange to me that when I open the cutlery drawer in my own house, I find only one set of cutlery.

When I was living at home with my mother, I once inadvertently bought a non-kosher frozen lasagne. After some discussion, we decided that, rather than let food go to waste, I would eat the lasagne on the patio and then re-kosher the fork I'd used by sticking its prongs down in earth for twenty-four hours (it was either that or immersion in a *mikvah**).

The first time my brother and I knowingly transgressed a law of *kashrut*† was when we were on holiday in Crete. He was seven and I was nine. Our hotel had a children's club and held a beach party for the kids staying there. Julian and I went along with the friends we had made at the swimming pool, watched as the fire was lit and accepted a sandwich each. Only when we had both already taken a bite did it occur to us to ask what was in them. The answer horrified us: ham and cheese! Not only milk with meat, but *pig* meat!

We looked at each other in terror, dropped the sandwiches and ran as fast as we could down the length of the beach and back

---

* A ritual cleansing bath.

† Jewish dietary law.

into the hotel complex, not stopping until we had reached our parents on their loungers by the pool. Breathlessly, we admitted our sin, and waited for whatever was coming to us. But God did not strike us down, and neither did our parents. All they did was to laugh at the drama we were making of it, and tell us to ask first next time.

⁎

'The rabbi can do the prayers at the house,' Mum says, 'but obviously he didn't know Julian, and he thought that since you're a writer, you might like to write a few—'

'No!'

'… words. Why not? You're a writer! It's what you do!'

'I'm a writer who's just lost her brother.'

'You might find it helpful.'

'I don't know about that.'

'Please – it would mean a lot to me… *please.*'

'Oh, all right, then.'

'*Thank you*, darling. I do appreciate it. I know you're grieving too.'

So we agree that I'll write the eulogy, but the rabbi will deliver it. Miserably, resentfully, I set about the task of writing a few words about my brother, in the voice of an unknown rabbi:

It would be impossible, of course, to sum up Julian's life in the short time available. Just over halfway through his

threescore and ten, he had already packed in so much of
value, and been so many things to so many people.

His professional field was bioinorganic chemistry, and he was,
by all accounts, an exceptional scientist. After gaining a first-
class degree in chemistry from the University of East Anglia,
he won a scholarship to Yale, where his research into the
chemical processes of photosynthesis led to the publication of
a paper in the journal *Science*, an extraordinary achievement
for someone so early in his career.

Julian completed his PhD, for which he won an award, and
then moved on to postdoctoral work at Berkeley, where he
met his wife, Ayako, and then at the University of California
in San Francisco. Four years ago Ayako and Julian both took
up assistant professorships at the University of _____ . He
was now managing his own lab, and his students have spoken
warmly of him as an adviser and mentor. His colleagues also
remember him with great affection and respect, and have told
his family that at the time of his death Julian was engaged,
as he always had been, in many exciting and innovative
projects. Recently he had succeeded in bringing a sizeable
and prestigious research grant into the lab. His students and
collaborators hope to continue his work.

Outside the lab, Julian was a loving husband to Ayako and an
indulgent father to his daughter Giselle. He also cared deeply
for his mother, Ruth, and sister Joanne, and for his many
friends. He missed his late father, Maurice, very much.

His family, friends and students all remember him as a warm
and generous person, a great wit, a fabulous cook and, after
a few drinks, a loveable buffoon. He loved to listen to music,

read widely, dressed well, ate well and was committed to
filling his house with beautiful things, and his kitchen with
every conceivable gadget.

He will live on in his work, his bright and beautiful daughter
Giselle, and in the memories of the many people who knew
and loved him.

Of course it is impossible, in the short time available, to sum
my brother up. There's a lot I have to leave out: the nature of
his death, for example, not to mention (no, *don't* mention) the
difficulties he was having at work, the fact that he had stopped
speaking at all to our mother, and would only do so guardedly
to me. I don't allude to the time Julian told Mum that, as far as
he was concerned, religion was just a way of making people feel
guilty.

He would have hated these prayers, but this is beside the point.
Mum explained to me when Dad died that funerals are a rite of
passage for the living. She needs these prayers to grieve for Julian,
to bring her family and her friends around her, to turn her loss into
the public property that losses are supposed to be. By holding
these prayers in the family home, under synagogue auspices, with
a rabbi and my uncles, the neighbours, all the old family friends
who have known him since he was born, my mother is folding
Julian back into the community he left – and that is one reason he
would have hated them, and why I'm finding them unbearable.

They're dragging him back and, worse than that, they're
making him dead – *officially* dead. The rabbi in front of me, my

uncle behind me, my mother with her arm linked through mine, are reciting the Kaddish, the prayer for the dead which says nothing about the dead except – by implication – how unquestionably right God is to take them away:

> Let us magnify and let us sanctify the great name of God in the world which He created according to His will. May his kingdom come, and His salvation flourish in your lifetime, and in your days, and in the lifetime of the family of Israel – quickly and speedily may they come. Amen.
>
> May the greatness of His being be blessed from eternity to eternity.
>
> Let us bless and let us extol, let us tell aloud and let us raise aloft, let us set on high and let us honour, let us exalt and let us praise the Holy One – blessed be He! – though He is far beyond all blessings, songs and honours that can be spoken of in this world. Amen.[*]

Or let us *not* extol, let us withhold our exaltations and refuse our praises. What do they all think they're doing standing here, in my mother's blessed through-lounge, rubber-stamping a death that never should have happened?

**

---

[*]   The Assembly of Rabbis of the Reform Synagogues of Great Britain (eds), *Forms of Prayer For Jewish Worship: I: Daily, Sabbath and Occasional Prayers* (London: The Reform Synagogues of Great Britain, 1977), p. 306.

Several times – more than several times – during my depressed and anxious teenage years, my mother asked me if I'd like 'to see someone' or 'talk to someone', but I always said no. I find it hard now to understand why I refused. I certainly didn't enjoy being unhappy. My best guess is that I resisted simply because it was my mother who suggested it. Whatever the reason, she didn't make me and I didn't go.

But my brother did. My memory of the timing of his treatment is hazy. It might have been when he was in the sixth form, following a horrible incident when another boy punched him at Harrow bus station while he was making his way home from school. That would have been an obvious reason, but I have a feeling that he had long since finished with the therapist by then. I do know what they talked about, and that was my brother's greatest fear, the one that stayed with him till the end, which was that he would 'wind up like Dad'.

To wind up like Dad was to be thwarted, to feel trapped and frustrated. It was to fail to do what you always wanted to do – in Dad's case, to be a scientist – and instead to take up a profession which your family chose for you and which you never enjoyed. It was to make bad judgements and have your superiors take advantage of you. It was to take refuge in childishness, cramming your face with sweet things and spending too much money. It was to express your frustration in fits of ridiculous, Basil Fawlty-ish temper, clenching your teeth and wringing your hands so hard that they squeaked. Often, during Julian's adolescence, he would provoke Dad or Dad would provoke him. I would hear them shouting, followed by the sound of my brother's big teenage feet pounding up the stairs and finally the slamming of his door.

The rows between our menfolk never worried me or Mum too much – we called them 'antler clashes' and saw them as a function of my brother's masculine growing pains – but they upset Julian terribly. He saw his own shouting back as a sign that he was turning into his father. So that was the concern he brought to his four or five sessions of therapy, and four or five sessions were enough to reassure him that he was not a replay, but his own self. At least, they seemed like enough at the time.

If my father's rages were ridiculous, it was because rage wasn't an emotion he could ever carry with conviction. He was a gentle soul, vague and impractical. In both those respects, I was always in more danger of becoming him that my brother ever was. Dad and I, Mum said, were 'hopeless and helpless'. It didn't matter how many times she showed us how something should be done – we always forgot.

And in some ways I am becoming even more like Dad. For example, he was a homebody; he adored his wife and children and hated being apart from them. In the last weeks before his sudden death, he was in excellent spirits because we were both due to visit at the same time. Julian was going to fly in from the States and I was going to come down from Scotland. For the first time in months, we were all going to be together in one place, at home. His last words, as Mum kept telling us afterwards, were 'Two more Mondays!'

*
**

Kathy comes to meet us in the Best Western lobby. She is the wife of one of the senior faculty members and we are going to spend much of the week in her care. As the days go by, I will come to think of her, with her perfect manners, deliberate speech and sweet white smile, as the essence of Plainsville. Long after my return home, when I think of those ten days, or of this place, two images always appear first, one imagined, one remembered: the imagined one is my brother lying down to die, while the remembered one is Kathy's mild, bespectacled, ever-smiling face.

Kathy's smile sets the tone for all our encounters: we are three nice, friendly ladies, one gracious hostess and two perfect guests, engaged in a marathon coffee morning, with just the occasional break here and there for a bout of hysterical grief.

This first morning, she takes us downtown for breakfast. She parks in a street parallel to the main street, a street entirely lined with churches. My brother once told me how sick he was of people asking them which one they were planning to attend. Well, there was certainly a wide enough choice.

Kathy leads us into a bakery café – the best place for breakfast in Plainsville, she says. As we look at our menus, she makes recommendations. I tell her how much I enjoy eating breakfast in the States.

'You have a national genius for it,' I say, and her smile widens gratefully. The waiter arrives, and the pair of them turn to the pair of us with great eagerness and some anxiety, as if they have just pitched a business venture, or asked us to marry them, and our responses could break them for ever.

'Have you made your choices?' she asks.

We have. We order the food. We eat it. We say how truly wonderful it is. But my coffee takes a while to arrive, and Kathy has to remind the waiter. When he brings it he is very apologetic.

'I'm so sorry it took so long,' he says.

I say it's fine and smile but my eyes must have something quite other in them, because the sympathy in his face and the consolatory squeeze he gives my shoulder are really quite disproportionate.

**

A traditional Jewish funeral takes place as soon as possible after the death, so my brother and I had to rush home the instant we heard. There was no time to digest the news: our father had not, as far as anyone knew, been dying, but today he was dead, so we had to pack bags, buy tickets and go.

I arrived first, to the home without our father in it, to our mother without her husband, to our grandparents without their son. I had my first big crying fit an hour later, when my mother told the rabbi that we would sit shiva in our house, 'because this was Maurice's home', and her sobbing set me off. Julian had his when he came through the front door the following day and he saw our grandfather's face.

'It's OK,' I said when I'd bundled my brother into the kitchen, 'I was the same yesterday. It's just the shock.'

'Did you cry on the way as well?' he asked.

'Yes, but not really sobbing, I sort of...'

'... leaked tears?'

'Yes, exactly.'

'Me too. All the way across the ocean.'

**

Kathy and her smile have been showing us around the campus. We have been admiring the university art gallery: its clean white spaces, the permanent collection of old masters from old Europe and the current special exhibition of antique quilts.

'That's lucky,' I say. 'Mum quilts, don't you?'

'Is that so, Ruth?' Kathy asks. 'What have you made?'

My mother shakes her head. 'Oh, I'm an amateur – I couldn't in a million years make anything like these.'

'She's made a couple of quilts for my son,' I say, 'which he loves.'

'They're a big part of your cultural history here, aren't they?' Mum asks.

'Yes,' says Kathy. 'They used to be quite overlooked, I think, but now people are coming to appreciate their value. It always makes me proud to see women's work celebrated.'

And they're off: they have found something in common, and between them they manage to stitch together a whole fifteen minutes of unforced conversation. It's a relief, and takes us all the way up to lunch, which we have at the campus food court. With its concession stands and plastic seating, it reminds me of the concourse at Addenbrooke's hospital, except that nobody here is sporting a stethoscope, or a drip. The clientele here are mostly young and healthy, and to my eyes, huge; not even fat – just big, well-nourished, *corn-fed*.

'The university has a reputation as something of a party school,' says Kathy. On the drive up we passed a long row of 'Greek Houses', where the members of fraternities and sororities sleep and socialize. I remembered a conversation I'd had with Julian years ago, when he was spending the middle year of his degree at the University of Massachusetts. I'd asked him about the tumultuous noise in the background.

'That's J.D. next door,' he'd said. 'He's a Frat Man.'

Now I tried to imagine him teaching all the Frat Men, the noisy Frat Men, who'd come here to party. I tried to insert my dry, English brother into this food court, moving among the white teeth and the athletes' shoulders and the backwards baseball caps, the burgers and the milk shakes, the 'Yo!'s and the 'Hey!'s. I can't do it with any conviction. The students eating their lunch around us, whom I will never speak to or lay eyes on again, can only be types to me, and when I try to place Julian in their midst he becomes a caricature himself, an Uptight British Professor, the

butt of jokes in a campus comedy called – well it would have to
be – *Party School!*

Party School!, starring the Two Football Players at the next table,
with the Tanned Girls In Shorts behind us as the love interest
and featuring Julian Limburg as the Uptight British Professor –
will he loosen up and give Main Football Player the grades he
needs to pass chemistry, or will he fail him again and lose him the
scholarship? Will that limey asshole ever crack a smile? Will he
ever realize this is *Party School!*?

⁑

They went down like ninepins: our father in September 1996,
his uncle – our grandmother's favourite brother – the following
month, then our grandfather in May, our aunt in July and our
grandmother in September 1997. Every time there had to be a
funeral, and Julian would have to take a plane eastwards to grieve
with everyone else and then take a plane back westwards to carry
on grieving alone.

Dad's sister, Auntie Marian, died only a few days after our
father's tombstone consecration (we call it a 'stone-setting'), so
on that occasion my brother was already in the UK. Marian had
been suffering from ovarian cancer for some months, but her
death, the timing and manner of it, was unexpected. The six of
us – our Uncle Brian, cousins Lisa and Nikki, Mum, Julian and
I – convened at our uncle's house at two in the morning, and
discussed arrangements. Mum, Julian and I were to drive over to

our grandmother's house at breakfast time, and tell her that her daughter was dead.

The car journey from our house to our grandparents' was one I had been taking once a week since I was born, and it had always been familiar and comforting, its different stages unfolding like scenes in a favourite bedtime story: the long fence by Whitchurch playing fields, the giant green gasometer at the bottom of Marsh Lane, Canons Park station, the road into Edgware with the pet shop, the second-hand bookshop, the salt beef bar; through Edgware to Apex Corner, then past big, beautiful houses to Mill Hill where there was a Chinese restaurant – the first I ever knew about – which had life-sized stained-glass ladies in its windows, whose gowns after dark on the way home would glow with a delightful warmth, and always made me think that they must be local deities there to bless and protect us on our way; Hendon Central with the huge cinema, Hendon Way, past Basing Hill Park, then right onto the Vale, right again, and left, where the house I still dream most about was the second one along, and neither it nor its iron gate, nor the roses in the front garden, nor the red brick steps up to the door, nor the two milk bottles I picked up, nor the lock my mother put her key to had any inkling of what was about to hit them.

Neither did Nanny. As soon as she heard the door she appeared at the top of the stairs and asked, innocently, 'What news?' My mother told her and the force of it bent her over double.

'Oh my God, oh my GOD! My whole family – wiped out!'

Mum ran up the stairs to take hold of her. I gasped and sobbed and ran into the dining room, where I stood with my back to the wall, hugging the milk bottles. Julian came in after me and put his hands on my shoulders. He was upset, but unlike me, he was calm, he had managed to keep part of himself available for someone else. He put his hands on my shoulders.

'Are you OK?'

I don't remember what I said. I do remember that he coaxed the milk bottles away from me and put them in the fridge. That was a useful thing to do. My brother was a useful, kind person, even when he was devastated. That's what I want you, the reader, to know about him.

⁎

Oh my God, oh my GOD! My whole family – wiped out!

While Julian and I were downstairs putting the milk away, my mother was upstairs with Nanny, trying to convince her that of course she hadn't done anything terrible in her life, that the appalling losses she'd had weren't any kind of divine punishment. Our grandmother was not an observant Jew, but in her extreme distress she couldn't help reverting to the biblical assumption that suffering results from transgression. Adam and Eve partake of forbidden fruit and are thrown out of Eden; Cain kills his brother Abel and is made to wander the world ever after, marked with his disgrace; David commits adultery with Bathsheba, brings about the death of her husband, and God punishes the couple by taking their first child. Jerusalem, the weeping woman of Lamentations, has 'grievously sinned, therefore she is removed' (1: 8). It is only Job who, like my poor grandmother, has done nothing to bring his agony on himself. And God's answer to him, when he finally breaks and asks why, can roughly be summed up in the following words:

BECAUSE I CAN.

So let us magnify and sanctify His great name, for He does whatever He likes.

**

If you'd heard my grandmother, you would have thought, as I did, that if God were real and just, her tears should have moved Him to pity.

In chapter 31, verse 15 of the book of the prophet Jeremiah, who was once assumed to have been the author of Lamentations, we can find the image of the matriarch Rachel, disturbed in her tomb at Ramah, weeping for her children. In the King James version, the passage reads as follows:

> 15. Thus saith the LORD; A voice was heard in Ramah, lamentation, and bitter weeping; Rachel weeping for her children refused to be comforted for her children, because they were not.

There is no mention of Rachel in Lamentations itself, but

she does feature in the rabbinical commentary on the book.
This commentary is vital to Jewish practice and belief. The text
of the Bible is somewhat laconic, even cryptic in places. Some
passages seem to contradict other passages. Others are extremely
ambiguous and give rise to conflicting interpretations. Biblical
narratives are often uncomfortably sketchy, riddled with gaps.
Characters and events are brought up and dropped again, their
stories left untold. The Bible offers us not a coherent story, but
the fragments of one.

Over the centuries, the rabbis worked to fill in the gaps.
Their work resulted in a huge body of literature, known as the
Midrashim. In a Midrash, the writer takes one biblical passage
and, using cross references to others, suggests plausible extra
scenes to fill the story out. The Midrash on Lamentations takes
the image of Rachel weeping from the Book of Jeremiah and
expands it into a story about the power of maternal grief.

In this story, Jeremiah leads God and his ministering angels
to Jerusalem to show them the full extent of its (or her?)
destruction. God weeps and calls on Jeremiah to summon the
patriarchs – Abraham, Isaac and Jacob, and, for good measure,
Moses – so that they can come out of their tombs to weep along
with their creator. Moses and the patriarchs are all, of course,
devastated by what they see; one by one, they plead with God
to show mercy to Israel, reminding Him of what they themselves
have done for love of their people, and out of obedience to
Him. Their lamentations move the ministering angels to weep

with them, but God will not relent: Israel has transgressed and the destruction of her Temple is the consequence of her transgressions. He even calls on the Torah and the letters of the alphabet to come and testify against Israel, before Abraham shames them into silence. Moses asks God how he can tolerate the slaughter of parents and children in one day, when the Torah expressly forbids it. God remains silent.

It is at this moment, according to Rabbi Samuel ben Nahman, that 'the matriarch Rachel [breaks] forth into speech' before God and reminds him of her own sacrifice, how she allowed her sister Leah to marry Jacob in her place, and then waited seven more years before she could marry him herself. She was kind to her sister who was her rival; she did not stand in her way or expose her to the shame of rejection.

> And if I, a creature of flesh and blood, formed of dust and ashes, was not envious of my rival and did not expose her to shame and contempt, why shouldest Thou, a King Who liveth eternally and art merciful, be jealous of idolatry in which there is no reality, and exile my children and let them be slain by the sword, and their enemies have done with them as they wished!*

Now, finally, God is moved to be merciful. The image of Rachel weeping which appears in Jeremiah is followed by His response:

---

* Rev. Dr A. Cohen (translator), *Midrash Rabbah, Lamentations* (London: Soncino Press, 1939).

16 Thus saith the Lord; Refrain thy voice from weeping, and
thine eyes from tears: for thy work shall be rewarded, saith
the Lord; and they shall come again from the land of the
enemy.

And so the gaps in the story are filled. Not by literal truths
that have been recovered, but by useable constructions that give
form to the intuited meaning behind the original text. Sometimes
we have to do that to make a story work, to prop a narrative
up and stop it from collapsing. Raw memory, like the Bible, is
often too laconic to make any sense by itself. In order to make
this story readable, for example, I have found it useful to take the
fragments of dialogue I truly remember and fill them out with my
own plausible constructions.

But that line of my grandmother's is no construction. I could
never make that up; nor could I ever forget it.

Oh my God, oh my GOD! My whole family – wiped out!

**

I am back at the house, sitting round the breakfast table with
Julian's postdocs, helping to pick out photographs to display at
the reception. My niece is in day care, my sister-in-law is resting
upstairs and my mother is back at the hotel: this is just me,
Lindsey, the postdocs and my absent brother.

The table is covered with pictures: my brother with Ayako at
Point Reyes, his favourite place; my brother with his newborn
daughter asleep in his arms; my brother and his toddler daughter

in a pumpkin patch, smiling together; my brother in Japan a few weeks ago, holding Giselle again, but this time looking away to one side, not smiling, not showing anything at all.

I pick up another picture. In this one, Julian is sitting down to breakfast at his in-laws' house in Osaka. I don't know which visit this was, but he does not have the disturbing, distant look I saw in the last pictures with his daughter. He is wearing a beautiful blue silk dressing gown, holding up a pair of chopsticks a little theatrically, looking straight into the camera and grinning. I know that grin, I've known that grin for ever and it shakes me like nothing else.

'Oh God, I can't believe it! Look at that face!'

Mum's not here, Ayako's not here – it's my turn to cry and have everyone come running.

*
**

After a year of flying back and forth to funerals, Julian fell ill. He was constantly tired, he ached, his glands were swollen and he kept running mild fevers. He was a PhD student at Yale at this point, and went to see the university doctors, who ran tests. They ruled out glandular fever, then Lyme disease, HIV and finally a pituitary tumour. This went on for a year while my mother worried and Julian fell behind in his research. In the end the doctors held a case conference and concluded that he was suffering from thyroiditis, but by then he was already beginning to recover, in the physical sense at least.

⁎⁎

Lindsey is taking Mum and me out shopping. First we go out to
a supermarket – a huge, mainstream barn of the kind my brother
never felt comfortable in. I remember him telling me about the
culture shock of his first visit to the Plainsville Walmart, with its
racks of guns and its car park full of overweight farmers loading
animal feed into their pick-up trucks. There is a local wholefood
co-op where he preferred to go, and it was outside that co-op that
he bumped into a colleague and had his last conversation.

This isn't Walmart – there are no sacks of feed, no guns – but
as we go in, I still experience that dreamlike jolt you get when
you walk into any foreign supermarket and find a place full of
familiar things, but arranged and packaged in unfamiliar ways, so
that everything seems ever so slightly out of kilter.

We take a trolley – a cart – and go to the fruit aisle, where the
goods are unpackaged, but seem no realer for it. There is a pyramid
of apples: huge, red and impossibly uniform. The bananas are as
yellow as the apples are red, and just as large too. The tomatoes
are like tennis balls, and any one of the melons could put your
back out, should you be daft enough to lift it. These big, shiny
fruits are pandering to the laziest of my prejudices, and I resent
them for it.

I see other, worse aisles, packed with exactly the kind of stuff
a snotty Brit would expect: humungous feedbags of sugary, fatty,
salty, corn-syrupy fodder. It's not for eating but for drugging
yourself with, and I should know because I've done it often

enough myself. My brother was an excellent cook, and careful about what he ate; I'm not. I don't respect my body enough. I don't respect my life.

Next, we go downtown. There's a shop called Hope & Glory that sells foods from home, and there is a consensus among the lab women that any memorial for Julian would be incomplete without a proper nod to his Britishness. We talk a little on the way. I try to explain to Lindsey how impossibly huge everything seems to me here – how wide the roads, how vast the sky, how extraordinary the distance between two ordinary parts of an ordinary town.

'I visited Julian a couple of times on the East Coast,' I say, 'but I've never been to the interior before.'

Lindsey is shocked, not at my admission but at the wording of it. 'I've never heard it called "the interior" before,' she says.

I really didn't mean to make it sound so *Heart of Darkness*.

Downtown is one long road of shops with a couple of smaller roads off it. Lindsey finds a parking place right outside Hope & Glory, and we go in. The particular strangeness of this shop is the obverse of the strangeness of the supermarket: here the dreamlike effect arises from the sight of familiar things shelved and priced as if they were rare and exotic. Since I have accidentally othered Lindsey on the way here, it seems only right that Mum and I should have our turn.

'Marmite,' Mum says, 'definitely Marmite sandwiches.'

'But I was always the Marmite addict,' I say. 'You want to

know what's ironic about that, Lindsey? It was always advertised as "the growing-up spread", but the two girls in my year at school who really liked it were me and another girl, who's about *so* tall,'and I place the side of my hand halfway up my forehead.

Lindsey smiles politely. 'That's funny. Anything else you'd like? Biscuits? Cakes?'

Mum and I exclaim at a shelf of Mr Kipling's cakes.

'French Fancies! We have to have those!' I show Lindsey. 'We went to our grandparents' every weekend, and they always served these at teatime. I liked the pink ones, Julian liked the chocolate flavour.'

'They always served the same thing,' Mum says, 'year after year.'

'And the same for lunch,' I say. 'Always beef – they just called it "meat" – roast potatoes and cauliflower.'

'That cauliflower!' Mum says. 'Their grandmother must have started boiling it on Thursday – it was practically liquid!'

How many times have we gone through this routine? Now would be the moment for Julian to do his impersonation of my grandmother:

'Hello, dear, would you like a meat sandwich? [No, thanks.] A Tunnock's tea cake? [No, thanks.] Jam tart? [No. I'm really not hungry.] You're not hungry? [No.] (*Pause*) So would you like some fruit, then?'

*
**

In the spring after our father died, Mum and I went to visit my brother in New Haven, Connecticut. That year my brother had extraordinary hair. He had his roommate clip it very short and then paint it with a succession of arresting designs: red with a black biohazard sign; white with a single red Picasso rose; a blue and green Earth globe. Julian attended our grandfather's funeral with a blue and green globe head, and got stopped and searched at the airport on the way home. It was the only time this ever happened to him, and we all agreed that it must have been the hair.

During our visit, Julian had a Mondrian head, with white, red and blue blocks separated by black lines. No one seemed thrown by it in New Haven – which is a student town, after all – but when we spent a day in New York we were met first by stares, and then by frowns or laughter, depending. An elderly lady came up to us in a kosher diner and harangued him:

'You need to do this to your hair? What does your mother think of your hair? Look at your sister – *she* doesn't have hair like that! Is it some kind of a *statement*? Are you part of a *cult*?'

✱

Kathy and her husband Don have invited us to supper at their home. It's a fine size, low and L-shaped, set a little back from the road. The garden is huge, like my brother's, and like my brother's it features a vast, improbably green lawn that a body would be unwise to tread upon. There is a wide patio around the house, so

I walk on that instead, following it round the corner to the edge of a beautiful pond, where carp are swimming under the lily pads, and blue-green dragonflies, like perfect, jewelled automata, whirr back and forth overhead. There's no need to pretend to enjoy this, so I take my sincere enjoyment back to Kathy and offer it to her, guest to hostess; it seems to make her happy, which is just as well, because it's all I've got.

We are five for supper: Kathy and Don, Don's mother, Mum and me. The food is good and plentiful, the conversation strenuous. Fortunately, there is a presidential election on the horizon, so we can talk about that. In another stroke of good fortune, Kathy and Don are Democrats, so there is no need to go to the trouble of politely disagreeing with them.

Don's mother is a Democrat too, 'But you don't trust Obama, do you, Mom?' Don says, loudly. His mother makes a sceptical noise and shrugs with her mouth. She doesn't say much, but then, Kathy told us that she has been blessed with seven children, so perhaps she's grown tired of all the noise.

'I know it's nothing to do with me,' Mum says, 'but I wanted Hillary.'

'Well, we wanted Hillary too,' says Kathy.

'But the problem with Hillary is that she comes with baggage,' says Don. 'At least, this way, it's a clean slate.'

'Well, we'll see.'

'Do people mostly vote Democrat in town?' I ask.

'In town, with the university, we're pretty liberal, yes.'

'But not in the state, I gather.'

'No, I'm afraid not.' Don shakes his head. 'Why these rural, blue-collar folks want to vote for a party that does nothing for them… it's frustrating for those of us who would wish them to vote otherwise.'

'But it's the social issues, isn't it?' Mum says. 'Abortion, and… you know, the social issues.'

'I guess it is.'

'It's not always easy to get a more liberal perspective on current affairs,' says Kathy. 'We watch the news on BBC World. That's the only way to find out what's happening outside the States.'

'Yes, we do love the BBC,' says Don, and everyone smiles. That's their gift back to us: hosts to guests.

Don is going to take us back to the hotel, by way of the frozen custard place; nobody can properly visit this town without sampling the frozen custard. It's an institution, the frozen custard. So he takes us to the frozen custard joint, which is in the edge city, a few hundred yards from the hotel. I choose a scoop of vanilla with hot fudge sauce, and it is one of the smoothest, sweetest, most supremely comforting substances I have ever spooned into my mouth. What with the frozen custard and the lack of news, you could live out your time here in blissful oblivion and not even know you were choosing to do it.

We sit at a table on the concrete forecourt, squinting against the setting sun, and Don tells us how sorry he is about Julian, what a talented scientist he was.

'It was such a shock to all of us. You know, we all went through it in our time, the tenure process, the appraisals and committees… we all go through it… it's just how you take it, I guess.'

He is looking away from us as he says this, his eyes a little unfocussed, as if he is trying to convince himself as much as anyone else.

'That thing he said,' says Mum, later, when we're saying good night, 'what was that – was he trying to tell us something?'

'I have no idea,' I say. 'I have no idea how to read what anyone's saying out here.'

'Like Shaw said—'

'… "divided by the barrier of a common language." I knew you were going to say that.'

'Well it's good to know at least *I'm* still predictable. Good night.'

'Night.'

Vessel Four

Q: Do Jews believe in life after death?

A: *There is no simple answer to this question. Judaism and mainstream Jewish teaching concerns itself largely with the more practical questions of how one should think and act in this life. There are many observant Jews who don't believe in life after death at all. Whether he believes in the hereafter or not, no Jew would ever suppose that the next life should be the focus of this one.*

There is, however, always the hope that the just distribution of reward and punishment so patently lacking in this life will be duly supplied in the World to Come.

Neither of my parents believed in the afterlife. My brother certainly didn't.

**

Mum and I have been delivered back to the house for one afternoon, to attend the informal memorial gathering. The Marmite sandwiches and French Fancies have been set out on the dining table, and the house has been decorated with flowers and many, many photographs. Lindsey is there, of course,

along with Erin and Becky. I sit down on the sofa nearest the basement door, where Ayako is sitting, and Giselle comes running up
to us, a lump of Play-Doh in her hand, which she holds out to me.

'Make a ball,' she says. I do as I'm told. 'She comes to you
instinctively because you look so much like Julian,' says Ayako.
Mum is hovering near us, and I can feel how desperately she
wants to smooth everything out with her daughter-in-law. It's a
relief to me that people start arriving before she gets to try.

Giselle isn't the only person who comes to me instinctively.
Colleagues, students, postdocs I've never seen in my life cross the
room to tell me how much they miss my brother. Some of them
hug me, usually without permission, occasionally without having
spoken first.

At one point I'm cornered by a postdoc and his smiling, silent
little wife.

'So you are a writer? I have a great gift for writing, so I could
have gone into that profession, but I chose chemistry instead.'

'How did you find working with my brother?'

'He was a good chemist, a good boss – a very good man.
As I was about to tell you, I did some sports reporting for the
newspapers back home…'

A little later, I have managed to shake off the postdoc, and am
sitting next to a long coffee table, poring over a pair of little photo
albums, which Becky and Erin have filled with pictures of Julian
smiling, holding his daughter. Becky comes to ask me how I am,
and to my shame I start to cry again.

'I just feel… I keep feeling like he must be stuck in some terrible place just now, and I have to rescue him and I don't know how… Do you think he's somewhere awful, do you think he's suffering?'

'No, not all,' says Becky. 'He was a good person. I'm sure he's at peace.'

She puts her hand over mine, and I think of the fish symbol dangling under her dashboard; if she believes he's at peace, that must mean that I should too. Becky wouldn't lie about that.

**

Although mainstream rabbinical Judaism has little to say about the afterlife, there is a rich folklore to fill in the gaps. There are tales of heaven, of angels and demons. The wicked are punished by being denied entry to the afterlife, and must spend eternity wandering 'the waste and the wild'. Some of these wicked souls become *dybbuks*, evil entities that possess the living and must be exorcised.

The good are rewarded. My mother once told me about an Isaac Peretz story, 'Bontsha the Silent'. Bontsha is a meek and undistinguished man, who spends the whole of his earthly life trodden underfoot, but after death is welcomed rapturously by the heavenly host and offered anything his heart desires. All he can think to ask for is a hot bread roll and butter. The angels themselves are shamed by the simplicity of his request. My mother said he reminded her of her Uncle Charlie. Charlie – whose given name, like Peretz's, was Isaac – worked in a sweat shop, survived the

First World War and spent the remaining decades of his working life as a lift attendant at the Moorfields Eye Hospital. After a day's work, he would go home to the council flat in Aldgate he shared with his sister Sadie. I only remember meeting him a few times. He was tiny, with very blue eyes, and he played the piano for us. After he died, we found the stash of notebooks he'd filled with jokes and cartoons: his unlived life. I took them home with me and I will never, as long as I live, throw them away. That's all the reward I can give him.

⁂

My self-imposed ban on writing about my brother doesn't last. It can't last. I have a life to go back to – here, in the present. I have a husband and a son. We are having work done on the house. I have a book to write and, also, for the first time in years, a job. At the end of September, just a few weeks after the event, I begin a two-year, part-time stint as a Royal Literary Fund Fellow at a Cambridge college.

I am there for two days a week, to help students with their writing skills. My duties are light, and for much of the time I am alone in my office, watching the swans on the Cam through the window, mostly working on my book, but occasionally writing notes about my brother. I know I swore I wouldn't, and shouldn't, but the words come into my head anyway, and buzz around painfully, so that I have to give them egress:

He was a baby, first of all.

He was a baby brother.

Mum says that after two weeks, I asked when he was going.

I can't bear it that he's gone.

He took the potassium cyanide and went and lay down on
the sofa ['couch'] in the basement, & quietly died. Why?

I said to S. on the phone, about the difference between him
& me, our different paths, our different futures, that you
can't express yourself through chemistry.

'But he did in the end,' she said, as unanswerable as he had
become.

The college encourages this, inadvertently, by commissioning
me to write a poem for an anthology of landscape poetry. As I
wouldn't know how to begin to write about a landscape I love,
I write about the landscape that's troubling me: the too-wide,
too-hot, too-bright landscape of the Midwest in summer. I
don't mention my brother in the resulting poem, but really it's
about nothing but him, and the writing of this first poem sets a
precedent. I've started and now I won't stop.

I'm grateful to the college for commissioning the poem, and
thereby giving me the permission I couldn't have given myself.
I'm grateful to them for the office, which I can use five days a
week. I'm grateful for how welcoming and helpful they are. But
the job does come with one complication: the need for childcare.
One day a week, I have to ask my mother to look after my child.

Which means that once a week she comes to our house, and I have to find ways of not talking about Julian. It means feeling guilty that I don't feel more grateful to her. It's easy to feel grateful to the college; with my mother, it's a different matter.

She looked after my brother's child, and he didn't like the way she did it; he stopped talking to her, and a few months after that he died. She's lost her confidence as both a mother and a grandmother. There is more riding on this routine babysitting job than it or either of us can bear.

It only takes a few weeks for the still-molten past to erupt through the screen of the present. One day, at school pick-up time, my phone rings.

'Hi, darling. It's me. I'm so sorry to phone, but I don't know what to do...'

'What's happened?' I'm imagining bullying, accidents...

'He's crying. He's sat down on the grass and he won't move. He says he won't go home without a playdate.'

Is that all?

'Oh dear, I'm sorry. He's been doing that a lot with me lately – it's a pain. Sometimes I give in and arrange something on the hoof but mostly I don't – and I shouldn't. I can't do anything from here, though...'

'I'm sorry, I know, but I didn't know what else to do...'

'Just tell him to go home with you, tell him there are biscuits there, tell him he can have a playdate another day, tell I'm I'll be home later – I'm sorry, but I can't be there.'

'I know. I'm sorry. I didn't know what else to do… Bye.'

I put the phone down, and it comes back to me, that conversation we had again and again:

'They were so angry with me because I left Giselle in the buggy – but she screamed every time I took her out – I didn't know what else to do… And when I turned up at the door with her, it was the same thing, I didn't know what to do. They just left her with me, and she didn't know who I was, she wanted her mummy and daddy!'

When I come home, my son is perfectly content, and my mother distraught. *I didn't know what else to do* has been tormenting her too. She wishes she hadn't used it again, that fatal form of words. I promise her it's fine, *we're* fine. I tell her of course she's not a bad mother or grandmother. I assure her I won't ever push her away.

*
**

A few days into our Plainsville visit, it's Boris's turn to take us to lunch. He is a newly tenured professor, Russian, and, rabbi aside, the only other Jew we meet in Plainsville.

'Julian was an exceptional scientist,' he says. 'He had a paper in *Science* when he was still doing his PhD – who does that? People go their whole careers without a paper in *Science*.'

'We're so proud of him… You have a bound copy of his thesis, don't you, Mum?'

'Yes. Pride of place – next to Joanne's poetry collections!'

'I can't understand a word of it,' I say, 'except for the jokes.'

'He put jokes in a chemistry thesis? Now that is *so* Julian – what were they?'

'There was a quote from W. C. Fields at the beginning,' I say. '"If at first you don't succeed, try, try again. Then quit. There's no point in being a damn fool about it."'

'And at the end,' Mum says, 'it's from a children's book – a Dr Seuss…'

'*The Berenstains' B Book.*'

'Yes, Joanne – right at the end of the story, on the very last page it says, "And that's what burst…"' I join in with her '…"baby bird's balloon!"'

Boris smiles, though we can't be making any sense to him.

'There was one more thing,' I say. 'He replaced one of the page numbers with a very small picture of a deer. No one noticed. He had to point it out to me.'

Our food arrives. When the waiter has gone, Boris leans forward.

'Listen,' he says, 'I have to tell you – I think I was the last person he spoke to, I was the last person outside the house who met him alive. Can I tell you?'

'Please,' says Mum.

'It was outside Whole Foods. I was on my way in, and I met him coming out. He seemed – I don't know – not himself, distracted, and I noticed he wasn't carrying any groceries – on the way *out* – and I remember thinking, "How strange", but we talked normally, normal stuff: he said he was just back from Japan, how was the trip, how was I, see you at work... you know... And then he went, and, and, well... It was just a normal conversation, you know?'

'Thank you,' says Mum.

'It was a surprise to everyone,' I said. 'There was nothing you could have done about it.'

'Of course not!' Mum cries. 'We didn't know, Ayako didn't know – nobody knew...'

'Thank you, thank you... I keep playing it over in my head.'

'I'm afraid you will for a while,' says my mother, the retired social worker. 'That's what happens. We're sorry.'

After lunch, Boris offers to show us round the faculty, the place where my brother spent most of his waking hours. It is a short walk from the main campus thoroughfare. We follow a zigzagging concrete path down to the bottom of the hill, to a solid, brown block that I could imagine finding in any university at home, except for the sign on the door:

Did that mean it was all right to carry them into your lecturers unconcealed, then stick them on your desk along with your pens and highlighters, your laptop and your take-out cup of coffee? My brother walked in past that sign every day. I wonder if it still seemed odd to him by the end – I can't believe it never did.

Boris takes us up to the labs first. He leads us down a long corridor that smells just like the science department at my old school. It's that pale orange smell with a hint of ammonia blue: apricots precisely on the turn. We pass a door with Ayako's name on it, then, a few feet along, we stop at my brother's door: his 'n' hers chemistry labs, mirror images. I remember now that they both have connecting doors into a shared office, where Giselle slept when she was still too small for day care.

The door with my brother's name on it opens into a long, light room, furnished with long benches and equipped with many machines. The ordering, procuring, installation and maintenance of these machines, without which the lab would grind to a halt, caused my brother much grief. I used to hear all about it over the phone: the slowness of the faculty administration, the laborious process of getting the necessary funds from finance, the suppliers who either sent the wrong machines or installed them incorrectly. On one occasion, I asked what the latest grief-machine was supposed to do.

'It heats up and then cools down very, very quickly,' he said, so that was me told, but still none the wiser. I used to long to talk to him about the research he loved, rather than the admin he hated, but then he would have had to find a way of explaining his work that was at once simple enough for me to understand and complex enough to do it justice, and there never was a way.

My brother's lab is still working without him, still peopled: one of his PhD students, Tim, is sitting at a bench at the front of the room, checking something on a laptop; Becky and Erin have been standing together at one of the bigger, free-standing machines that line the wall, and come over to greet us. They show us around, doing their best to explain what goes on here, pointing out the more impressive machines, taking every possible opportunity to assure us how all the good work that they did here flowed in one way or another from my brother's efforts. He was so smart; he was such a good boss; he really set the tone.

'What's that?' I point to an enclosed area by the back wall, with clear Perspex sides. I would have said that it was a fume cupboard like my school chemistry teacher used to show us the experiments which were too messy or dangerous or expensive for us to do ourselves, except that one side has three sets of arm-holes, from which three pairs of long, clear gloves hang down into the space.

'That's where we do certain experiments when we have to be extra careful not to contaminate the materials,' Erin says, as we walk over to it.

'Because we're working with the DNA,' Becky says, 'using catalysts.'

'Speeding up evolution?' I ask, before I remember that Becky would never put it like that.

'No. That wouldn't be possible,' she says.

.:.

It was October 1995. I had yet to move to the comfortable flat overlooking Holyrood Park, and was living instead in a much more squalid one in the west end of Edinburgh, working part time for a broadcast monitoring company and writing poems. Julian was thousands of miles away, in New Haven, trying to figure out how to replicate photosynthesis.

During one of our long phone calls, I told him about a poem I was writing: it was about a woman who always 'had to rein in her desire / to fix a thing / before its fixing time' and in it I set up a rather heavy-handed analogy between the process of setting up experiments to get a particular result or reaction and that of looking for the right partner. The particular line I wanted to check with him was '… time after time / the solution remained in suspension'.

He put me straight. 'That makes no sense. Something's either a solution or it's in suspension. It's got to be one or the other.'

So I gave up on the poem – which was terribly laboured anyway – and set to writing another. My brother went back to his bench, and the long process of trying, getting nothing, getting nothing, getting nothing, then trying again. He did get there in the end, and I learned from his example.

.:.

Just outside the lab we're joined by Debbie, a chemistry major whose final-year project my brother was supervising. In a town of wide smiles and white teeth, she has the widest and the whitest. I smile back, but what I really want to do is to stick my hand over my British mouth.

Julian was a great teacher, she says. Julian was so caring to his students. And so *funny*.

'Like, I'm just looking at the safety shower now,' she says. She nods towards a rickety-looking tank that's fixed to the wall in a recess just by the lab door. It has a chain hanging down from it, like an old-fashioned lavatory cistern. 'Do you remember that time with the safety shower, Erin?'

'Oh yes.'

'You see, I had an accident,' Debbie says, 'a spill, and got this quite noxious stuff all over me, on my clothes and my shoes, and the faculty regulations say, if that happens, you should run out and stand under the safety shower, and pull the chain…'

'But look at it!' Erin says. 'No one has pulled that chain for years – no one remembers anyone ever pulling it—'

'… so the water in there is kind of—'

'… it's never been cleaned, either, so – you can imagine – it's *funky*.'

'So I came out here, and I was standing just where you are, and I was looking at the mouldy old tank, and Erin came out too, and we were trying to decide, and then Julian came out to see what was the matter, so we asked him, and he said – what was it he said? It was just kind of the *way* he said it...?

'He looked at Debbie, then he looked up at the tank just for a moment, and then he said, "Well, you *could* stand under it and pull the chain if you *want* to, but I probably *wouldn't.*"'

'It was the way he said it,' said Erin, and they laugh together.

'I can just hear him saying it,' I say. I can, and it is very funny.

We say goodbye to the lovely, laughing chemistry girls; it's time to visit the faculty offices, where no one ever got my brother's jokes. It is a couple of floors below the lab. The admin staff come out of their cubicles to meet us, all smiles and condolences. We accept both nicely, although we know perfectly well that my brother found these women impossible to deal with, and that the feeling was probably mutual.

Beyond the last cubicle, we find the chair of the faculty, a big man in a big job, filling the doorway of his office. He offers his hand to me and I take it, from as far away as I can.

'It's good to meet you,' he says. 'So sorry about the circumstances. Such a tragedy.'

He's twice my size, but when I meet his eye I could swear I see some fear in it. It's as if he thinks I'm concealing weapons.

∗∗

The book I'm writing at the time of Julian's death is called *The Woman Who Thought Too Much*, and it's a memoir about my own mental health issues, my anxiety and OCD. It isn't just the outside pressures, the contract and the advance that are driving me (my publishers are quite willing to give me a break and put the deadline back), but also my own need to finish a project that I've started, in which I've already invested so much of myself. (See my brother at the bench, trying and failing and trying again…) Poetry never feels like a proper day job to me – poetry flits, it comes and it goes – but this book-length piece of prose that I've been shaping and adding to for a couple of years has become an established, stable part of my life. I need that stability.

My brother haunts the book, but mostly by his absence. In writing this book about anxiety, I have discovered various fresh reasons to be anxious, one of these being the possibility that I might expose someone other than myself in a way that might hurt them. My strategies for avoiding this are to mention other people as little as possible, and to do my best to portray them in a not-too-unflattering light when I do. When I write about my mother, I emphasize her strength, her good intentions, how much she did to help and encourage and protect us, how much I must have tested her patience. I allude to her own anxiety only briefly, and do not mention her obsessive tendencies at all. I don't say how anxious she was for me to succeed, how much she overvalued my academic intelligence, how critical she could be. I certainly don't mention what she said on the night of my first period. Quite apart from the fact that my mother is alive and I don't want to hurt her, I am aware that memoirs in which parents are blamed or exposed are seen as a form of bad behaviour, and I need to be good.

It should have been easier to keep my brother out of my story – no one ever said 'They fuck you up, your brothers and sisters' or 'I blame the siblings'. No one would ask about the influence of a younger brother, well and well-behaved. He was never thought to be a problem. Unlike his sister. But now his sister is writing a book about mental illness, and he has presented her with a problem. I would rather not write about his suicide, but I have written about all my other losses and I feel it would be dishonest, *weaselly*, to leave this one out. I add a final chapter, undoing the neat ending I had planned to write. In as few words as possible, I recount the story of my brother's last months and I make sure to tell the reader, explicitly, exactly how much of a 'stupid, selfish woman' I have been, how I should have visited him, listened better, tried harder to be the sister he deserved.

**

Sometimes my mother's anxiety was completely justified; sometimes my brother and I did stupid things. I remember one instance when we were still very young – we couldn't have been more than ten and eight respectively – and I thought that it would be nice to surprise our parents by mowing the lawn for them. The shed was never locked, so we were able to take out both lawnmowers, the new electric one and the old-fashioned push mower, which meant that we could both mow at once, and get the job done quicker. I gave the push mower to Julian, plugged in the electric mower in the kitchen, and started work. Mum came out very shortly afterwards to find me attached to a mower on the end of a very long flex, and Julian attached to a piece of unearthed metal hardware close by. She screamed at us.

'What the *hell* are you doing? Don't you realize how *dangerous* this is? You could both be *electrocuted*! Do you think you'd look *good,* lying all *cold* and *blue* on the grass? Do you think you'd look *pretty*?'

*
**

That first summer after Julian's death, the three of us go to stay with my cousin David and his family in Hamburg. He is my mother's younger nephew, and there is a strong family resemblance: he could easily pass for my brother, or for Julian's. They were similar in other ways. They had the same gentleness about them, the same thoughtful air. And they both married non-Jewish women.

I remember their wedding very well. It was in a pretty hotel, just outside Frankfurt. I was going out with Chris at the time, and we had already agreed that I should move in with him, but as we weren't actually engaged, my aunt and uncle didn't think that it would be appropriate to add him to the guest list. So I went without him and shared a hotel room with my mother. My cousin's wife was mortified when she found out. Her family were very welcoming to David, and to the rest of us. All the wedding speeches were made in English as well as German. The bride's Finnish mother and aunts circulated after the meal, with red cheeks and enormous smiles, pressing tumblers of Finnish vodka on anyone they could corner. It wouldn't be a wedding without vodka, they said. It's for the couple! It's for luck!

On the last full day of our visit, we all take a train to Timmendorfer Strand, on the Baltic Coast. It is cool and overcast, and a fine rain is falling. It could be any beach in England, except that my cousin has to pay for admittance, and when he does the attendant asks if we are 'textiles' – in which case we should go to the right, as the nudist beach is on the left.

'Surely not in *this* weather!' I say, but when we look to the left, there they are, pale as unshelled oysters, striding into the water.

When I reach the shoreline, I realize the nudist swimmers are even tougher than I supposed. As well as braving the freezing water, they have to negotiate a dense smack of jellyfish – moons and lion's manes – suspended at the water's edge, going in and out with the tide. Dead or alive or a mixture of both, it's hard to tell. They are in all respects the most *between* creatures imaginable, neither flesh nor water, neither beached nor fully afloat, unable to move but never quite at rest. They have become their own element, and are trapped there, in a gelatinous neither/nor, a jellyfish limbo.

*
**

The funeral home here in Plainsville provides a complete package, which includes bereavement counselling. Kathy is keen for Mum and I to take advantage of this service – especially as my sister-in-law has refused to – so we have let her take us back to her house, the better to be counselled.

The counsellor is there already, a gentle, pastel cloud of a woman in a flowing linen suit. She offers us her condolences; we accept them. I have a suspicion that, should I say anything I really need to say, it would be like throwing a bucket of blood all over the pastel linen, so I let my mother do the talking. After several days of conversing with sympathetic strangers, she has developed a good, working narrative and now she rehearses it again: she knew something wasn't right; he must have been in such pain; she keeps thinking that this is just an awful nightmare and she'll wake up; if he turned up at her door now, she'd want to throttle him, and then give him the biggest hug in the world…

Something small and iridescent flutters at the window.

'A hummingbird!' I can't help it. 'I just saw a hummingbird!'

'Really? Where?' I think Mum is glad of the distraction.

'There. Against the window – over by the pond.'

'Oh yes, we have hummingbirds here,' says Kathy. 'Do you not have them in the UK?'

'Only in zoos. You're so lucky. They're such beautiful things.'

The counsellor takes a thin, glossy book out of her bag. It's the book of memories provided by the funeral home for the bereaved to use at the memorial service: there are places for photos of the deceased, headings in curly print to help prompt mourners, and, also in curly print, comforting and inspirational thoughts.

'No,' I say. 'This is… lovely. But it doesn't quite fit – not the situation, and not my brother. I'd rather we didn't… Sorry – no. Mum?'

'I agree with Joanne.'

Kathy and the counsellor both look disappointed, and it feels unkind to refuse the book, but this is my brother we're talking about, and I won't have his memory peachwashed.

**

Some months later I'm at the Lucy Cavendish College English department dinner. I have several friends who are alumnae (there are no alumni – the college admits only mature female students), and for the second year running they have invited me as their guest. Some of their partners are here too. One of the Lucy women I know is married to a psychiatrist. Last year, the psychiatrist and I had a fascinating conversation about OCD. This year we're talking about suicide.

'I've been reading about it,' I tell him, 'and apparently suicidality – I mean a suicidal state, not suicidal ideation – apparently it's not the same as depression? It can occur with it or without it – have I got that right?'

'You have, that's quite true. Suicidality is an altered state—'

'You mean the "cognitive constriction" thing?'

'Yes, there is that narrowing of the focus of the attention, but what I was going to say was that suicidality can actually be chemically induced.'

'Really? I didn't know that. How?'

The psychiatrist tells me a story about a very senior psychiatric research professor who took a particular drug, then shut himself in a room with nothing harmful in it, and instructed his team not to bring anything harmful to the room, even if he begged. As the professor had predicted, he became desperate to put an end to himself, by any means, and had to be restrained until the effects of the drug wore off.

'I don't know what medication my brother was taking,' I tell him. 'I do wonder about it.'

'Even if you knew what he was taking, it still wouldn't give you an answer as to why he did it.'

'I know... I know what it is to be very, very depressed, and not to see the point – it's what I've written about in the book... and he knew that. I feel so hurt that he didn't share how he was feeling with me.'

'I'm afraid suicidal people often shut themselves off.'

'I know – I've read about that too – but I wish I could have said to him, "I know what it's like not to see the point – I know what it's like to feel more dead than alive..."'

'"More dead than alive" – that sounds like Cotard's syndrome. Have you heard of that?'

'Is that the one where you think your loved ones are imposters?'

'No, that's Capgras' syndrome. Patients who suffer from Cotard's syndrome have the delusion that they don't exist, or that they're already dead, or bits of them are missing or rotting away… Sometimes they think everyone around them must be dead too, because they're in some kind of netherworld.'

I picture the jellyfish on the Baltic shore, washing in and out.

'I've often felt that, metaphorically.'

'Well if you ever felt it literally, that would be Cotard's.'

I look around the college dining hall at all the bodies, which could be empty automata for all I know, picking up forks and putting them down again, and I think of myself, how I've been moving through the days without my brother with the feeling that this is all posthumous, that life after my brother is gone can only be afterlife, and I know these are only metaphors, but they are the element I'm trapped in, my own gelatinous neither/nor.

⁎

There are decisions to be made: flowers, for the memorial reception on campus. Kathy takes us on another outing, this time to a florist's shop – the best – the university uses them, the funeral home, everybody uses them – and it's run by a very nice lady.

The shop feels like a hothouse: long, narrow and humid, blooming goods on all sides leaning in and overhanging. We shake moist hands with the proprietor in the small space her flowers have allowed her, and she shows us her funeral brochure.

'May I ask, what were Julian's favourite flowers?'

Mum and I exchange blank glances. Kathy steps in. 'Ayako has said white English roses. Is that right?'

'I have no idea,' Mum says. 'I'm sure Ayako knows best.'

'If you think we should use them, do,' I say.

'Yes, yes,' Mum adds. 'Do. That sounds lovely.'

Then there is the brochure to look at, fat with laminated photographs of wreaths, arrangements, glossy coffins and big, white smiles. *Smiles!* The florist points at one particular image, of flowers arranged around a beaming headshot of the deceased.

'Often our clients like to provide us with a picture of their loved one to—'

'No!' Mum and I speak at once, then Mum starts to apologize, and I run out of the shop.

*
**

Before Julian died, Chris and I were planning to have some major work done on the house. We understood that it was going to be disruptive, and that we would need to move out for a while. That was then, before the catastrophe. Now that Julian is gone, all I want is to curl up and hide in a familiar place, and I can't bear the thought of being turfed out of it. But I fail to get this across to Chris, so the work goes ahead. Shortly after Christmas, we leave our home with our cats and two vanloads of our possessions, and move into a rented house round the corner, opposite our son's school. I move the books I need for my research to my office at the college, and box up the rest. I hate being away from them. I hate the disruption to my work. My brother is dead, my mother is selling the family home, and now I am being displaced from yet another home, which is having the innards knocked out of it.

As I don't realize quite how thoroughly I've failed to make my feelings clear, I resent the building work and all that comes with it. I feel, quite unfairly, that Chris has pushed me into this when I am not ready. When we come to talk about it, years later, I will discover that, in his version of events, we were both of us keen to get on.

That first winter, I live in a world stripped out. Our rented house is a three-bedroom modern box with laminate floors and white-painted walls. It's comfortable, it's convenient, but the few bits of furniture we've brought over aren't enough to make it look like home. It's a way station, a holding place, another uncomfortable neither/nor.

Not everything is in suspension though: Mum can still visit us, I can still get irritated by her, she can continue to talk about my brother, and I can continue to change the subject. One day Chris hands me a letter from the States, a thank-you note from a friend of Julian's who's set up a trust fund for Giselle, acknowledging a contribution from me. It's written on the back of a long, thin postcard. On the front there's a picture of my brother, obviously very recent. He's smiling widely into the camera, holding Giselle up with both hands, while she points at something ahead and to the right, something exciting and interesting that her father has lifted her up to see. Underneath the picture, there are a few lines thanking the recipient for their generous gift to Giselle's 'educational trust fund', then a small space, then a couple more lines:

in memory of her father

JULIAN LIMBURG, 1972–2008

When I look at the dates, the familiar form of them on the page, the way they appear to balance each other on either side of the dash, I feel the same outrage as I did when I heard the Kaddish said in the family home. My brother's life is over, but that doesn't make it a life completed. I cannot bear to see it recorded as if it were. All the same, it's a beautiful picture, and I put it on the mantelpiece.

That weekend, Mum comes to visit. She takes herself and her many bags into the living room, while I go into the kitchen to put the kettle on. Then I hear a loud sob. Chris pokes his head through the kitchen door.

'I think your mother's found the card,' he says.

She has collapsed onto the sofa. I put my hand on her shoulder and let her cry it out, agree that it's terrible, it's wrong, Giselle should have a father, he must have been in such pain, if only Ayako would talk to her. I say I don't really know why Ayako won't talk to her, I say Ayako's in a lot of pain herself, she just can't cope with it, why should she blame you? And what about me?

Well, what about me?

'Oh, you know,' I say. 'In the end, he was the only one who did it. Who can say why?'

'When we're together, I feel as if Julian's the elephant in the room,' she says.

'You lost a son and I lost a brother,' I say. 'They're different losses, we're dealing with them in different ways.'

The night after she leaves, I can't sleep, so I go into the spare room where Mum has been staying. It's the barest room in a bare house, with nothing of ours in it but the folding bed that fits under our son's bed at home. I look out of the window, watch the snow falling through the orange sodium light, falling onto the wide, empty streets between the house and the primary school, blanking out the divisions between road and verge, verge and pavement, pavement and garden, stripping out the view to match the interior.

I keep thinking about my brother, the smiling father in the picture, the elephant in this and every room. He wanted to disappear from our view but all he did was make the opposite happen. My brother, who found a way to imitate photosynthesis in his PhD, to produce oxygen in a way it had never been produced before, whose friends made him a cake that said 'Jules, Maker of Oxygen', chose in the end to take a substance that would prevent the cells in his own body from taking any more oxygen in.

'My brother, the Oxygen Man,' I think. And words come into my head:

> It is your own good stuff,
> so breathe it, breathe it in.
> Blue is not your colour –
> let everything be green.

If I had my notebook to hand, I could write them down and then they would leave my head. But my notebook's in the other bedroom and I don't want to disturb Chris by going in to fetch it, so I can only let the words repeat at me, again and again, until they make me cry.

Vessel Five

Q: On Yom Kippur Eve, we are supposed to ask forgiveness from those we have sinned against. But what if the person we have injured is dead?

A: *In that case, the person seeking forgiveness must go to the graveside of the injured party and make his confession in front of ten witnesses.*

**

Yom Kippur, the most holy day of the Jewish calendar, is the culmination of the High Holy Days, the Ten Days of Awe that begin with Rosh Hashanah. It opens a once-a-year window for Jews to confess, beg forgiveness and get their moral accounts in order, ask please that their names be written in the Book of Life. Not in the other book. Of course, there is another book.

Jews do not, as Christians are instructed to,[*] go into their closets to do their spiritual accounting. They go out, to the synagogue,

---

[*] 'But thou, when thou prayest, enter into thy closet, and when thou hast shut the door, pray to thy Father which is in secret; and thy Father which seeth in secret shall reward thee openly.' Matthew 6: 6.

where the Torah scrolls will be covered in white cloths, the colour of the plain shrouds in which every member of the congregation will one day be buried, and they confess together. It's not meant to be a fun day, and I never found it so, but I used to rather enjoy the communal confession. It had a certain drama:

> We have abused and betrayed. We are cruel.
>
> We have destroyed and embittered other people's lives.
>
> We were false to ourselves.
>
> We have gossiped about others and hated them.
>
> We have insulted and jeered. We have killed. We have lied.
>
> We have misled others and neglected them.
>
> We were obstinate. We have perverted and quarrelled.
>
> We have robbed and stolen.
>
> We have transgressed through unkindness.
>
> We have been both violent and weak.
>
> We have practised extortion.
>
> We have yielded to wrong desires, our zeal was misplaced.[*]

I would look around the *shul* at everyone chanting – the men in their suits and prayer shawls, the women in their hats

---

[*] The Assembly of Rabbis of the Reform Synagogues of Great Britain (eds), *Forms of Prayer for Jewish Worship: III: Prayers for the High Holydays* (London: The Reform Synagogues of Great Britain, 1985).

– thinking how implausible it was to suppose that any of these familiar, respectable and – to me – *dull* people could ever have done anything as exciting as rob, steal, be violent or kill. I thought robbery was something career criminals did, with knives and crowbars, and that killing meant murder. I had an imagination, but it was full up with other worlds, with time travel, Regency beaux, dead pop stars and dead poets; when it came to the world I actually lived in, I had little or no capacity to imagine what it might be like to experience it as anyone but myself.

One thing I must have realized was that everyone was hungry. Yom Kippur entails a twenty-five-hour fast, commencing on the eve and ending at the following sunset. If the synagogues are full to bursting during the day, it is partly because people are hoping that attendance might distract them from thinking about food. Outside my enjoyment of the dramatic confessions, that never worked for me. And there was little other distraction possible at home or anywhere else. On Yom Kippur you cannot read anything but the prayer book. You cannot write. You cannot watch television, listen to the radio or play music. You cannot make phone calls. You cannot do any kind of work. You cannot handle money.

You shouldn't drive either, though our father used to drive us all to the synagogue in the morning. He would stay there all day, and sometimes our mother would too. Once my brother and I were old enough, we would walk back home after the morning service: it used up a whole hour. We would get home at about one, and then face the problem of how to fill six more hours…

'I'm thinking about chicken,' one of us would say.

'Shut up! Roast potatoes!'

'Cauliflower!'

'Lemon meringue pie!'

'Challah!'*

'Cheese!'

'No, we really have to stop it now.'

What could we do? We couldn't play Monopoly, Mum had told us, because of the toy money. We decided that we could play cards, as long as we confined ourselves to Snap and to Pairs, as no money was involved. We were allowed to play Trivial Pursuit, so we usually did.

One year someone lent us a special Jewish version of the game, with questions about the Torah, law and tradition, Jewish history, famous Jews and Yiddish wisdom. For the wisdom questions, you had to complete an English translation of one the wise sayings, for example:

'A rich man's daughter is always _____?'

'A beauty.'

It was a slow game – we were very bad at it. We were particularly bad at the Yiddish wisdom, and made very bad guesses. An hour or so in, I landed on yet another Yiddish saying square.

'Go on,' I said to Julian. 'Read it out. I won't get it.'

_____

*   A sweet plaited loaf, eaten on the Sabbath.

Julian picked a card out and read: '"Your health comes first
_____?"'

'"Your health comes first... Your health comes first" – nope,
nothing, no idea. What is it?'

Julian turned the card over, and burst out laughing.

'What? What is it? What does it say?' He passed me the card,
and I read aloud:

'"Your health comes first: you can always hang yourself later."'

And then we were both laughing.

*
*

My sister-in-law wants to talk to me. We're sitting next to each
other on the sofa, and for the first time we are alone.

'That afternoon here,' Ayako says. 'They ignored my wishes.
I didn't want all those photos everywhere, and the food they got
– Julian hated that kind of food.'

'I'm sorry,' I say. 'I'm afraid I chose some of it.'

'No, no, I don't mean the British stuff! That was nice. It was
the other things – cake. And neighbours keep bringing these
casseroles. I've said not to, I don't eat them...'

'I'm sure they only mean to be kind.'

'Oh yes, yes, of course, but they are so *Midwestern* – there's
only one way to do things.'

'I kept getting hugged by people who don't know me. They
didn't even ask.'

Ayako shudders. 'I know – I hate that.'

I tell her about the postdoc who talked at me that afternoon, the gifted writer with the silent wife.

'Ugh, Julian *hated* that guy – he said he was so self-important, you couldn't tell him anything... Listen, listen... About your mother—'

'It's OK—'

'But I just want to say, I'm sorry you both had to leave like that, but I just couldn't stand having your mum here. That morning, after you went to the shower, straight away she started talking to me about the money Julian owed. She always used to upset Julian about money – I couldn't bear it, he would cry. There was one time when Julian had offered to refund her plane ticket, and she started going on about it the minute she landed – on and on and on about it. She marched him to the cashpoint and she stood over him while he got the money – she stood over him!'

'I'm sorry, she didn't mean to be hurtful – she got very anxious about money, that's all.'

'Julian couldn't take it any more – every time he spoke to her, it was, "When will you repay the money?" He was so stressed, he was so stressed at work, he didn't need that pressure from her.'

'I didn't know why he borrowed it.'

'I don't know why either, but Julian was terrible with money – he was always coming home with new clothes, stuff for Giselle... He was feeling bad, he would buy something to make himself feel better, but it only made things worse...'

'Our dad was like that – Julian said he was scared of winding up like him. Oh dear.'

'He didn't need the stress from your mum – he had so much to deal with at work.'

'I'm sorry.'

'It's not your fault. He never said anything bad about you. He loved you.'

'I know it was difficult for him at work…'

Ayako tells me about Julian's work, about the members of the faculty who voted against his getting tenure despite the good work he was doing, despite the huge grant he brought in.

'That grant he got, you know, people try for years and years and they don't get it.'

I tell Ayako that we've been spending a lot of time with a faculty wife.

'Kathy – oh God, she thinks everything is her business. She's a midwife, and when Giselle was born she kept visiting us at the hospital and asking about breastfeeding, and then after we got home, she got all the other faculty wives to keep phoning me and visiting, asking how the feeding was going, checking up on me…'

'Perhaps it was meant to be supportive…?'

'It didn't feel that way. We just wanted to be left alone.'

It occurs to me that Ayako never asked us to come over here either. Mum and I are invading her space and intruding on her grief, and I don't know why. There's no funeral to attend, and nothing we can do to help. We're just creating work for people.

⁂

At some point in the months before my brother's death, I was telling my therapist about Mum and Julian and the money, how I was sick to death of hearing her talk about it.

'From the way she talks,' I said, 'you'd think she was going to be on the streets, but that's hardly going to happen. I wish she would just let it go for a bit.'

My therapist replied that money was never just money.

'Mum was poor,' I said. 'I guess once you've been poor, you're always poor in your head. The money's her security.'

I remembered a story my uncle told me. Twice a year – at Passover and Rosh Hashanah – he and my mother would take the bus from their overcrowded, semi-detached house in Cricklewood to a mansion block opposite St John's Wood, where they had well-to-do relatives. They would go round to the back of the building – *always* the back, because those were their instructions – where someone would come to the tradesmen's entrance and hand them a chicken and a bottle of wine, their seasonal bounty.

'Then every year,' my uncle said, 'they would say, "If you ever need anything, don't hesitate to ask", but when one day I did need something, and for once I decided not to hesitate, I didn't hear a thing back – nothing.'

And they never got invited in. Not once. The charity would be handed over on the doorstep, the empty promise made, and then they would be sent back to Cricklewood, to the house of poor relations.

⁎⁎

And what was the money to my brother? I've come to think that for him it was my mother's unconditional love, which he felt she withheld. Mum wanted the money back so that she could feel secure; for Julian to feel secure, he needed to hear that he could hang on to the money indefinitely, that it had been given to him without conditions, without strings. The result was an inevitable impasse.

⁎⁎

He never said anything bad about you. He loved you.

My parents used to tell me that when Julian was a toddler he would wake up in the morning calling for 'Dadoes'. My father would go into his little room and my brother would shake his head.

'*No*. Want *Dadoes*!'

Then I would go in, and Julian's face would break into the most enormous smile: ''*Ere-are* Dadoes!'

He had never known life without me. He loved me. In the last years of his life, before he stopped talking to me, he would often ask, apparently casually, if I might like to come over and visit with my family and – you know, just hang out…? I've always been a nervous traveller, and became more nervous at the prospect of travelling with a small child. I always said I'd think about it, but I never went. A better sister might have got over herself and gone. A better sister would've realized that she was needed.

∗∗

If only I had been a better sister, a better daughter... If I had only tried harder to reconcile them, if I had not held back a part of myself, then maybe...? When the Daughter of Zion weeps in the Book of Lamentations, she weeps not only from grief, but also remorse. Through her transgressions she has brought down the wrath of God upon herself, and it is this that is the cause of her ruin. 'The Lord hath afflicted me in the day of his fierce anger... The Lord is righteous; for I have rebelled against his commandment: hear, all people, and behold my sorrow...' God's patience has its limits too.

∗∗

Julian had a security blanket, and I did my best to part him from it.

It was one of those yellow open-weave cot blankets with satin edging. My brother would hold it all bunched up in one little fist, while he sucked the index and middle fingers of the same hand. At one point, he clutched two other blankets along with it, but he soon reverted back to his yellow favourite, which my father christened 'Mr Germy'. I remember how it used to trail after us round Sainsbury's, gathering dust.

Our mother was a social worker who had read Winnicott and had strong views about the importance of the transitional object. She always insisted that my brother would give the blanket up when he was ready to, and as it turned out, she was quite right: on the day that he started school, my brother ditched it, announcing that he was a big boy now and big boys didn't carry blankets. It was, however, a replacement Mr Germy that was discarded.

There were other relatives – mostly on my mother's side of the family – who didn't agree with her; Ruth should really take that blanket away from him, they said. Is he going to be dragging it around with him at school? To work? Down the *aisle*, for goodness' sake? I think I must have overheard them, because one day, when I was perhaps five and my brother three, I sidled up to him and we had the following conversation:

'You're a big boy now, aren't you?'

He nodded, fingers in mouth, blanket in fist.

'And big boys don't carry blankets, do they?'

He paused, then nodded again.

'So come with me. Come into the kitchen.'

He followed, and then, somehow, I persuaded him to hand me the blanket, and right in front of him, right there, I took the big scissors with the yellow rubber handles, cut Mr Germy up into little squares and threw them into the plastic swing bin. I remember thinking that this was for his own good, that he didn't know how he ought to conduct himself. But he can't really have understood the implications of what was going on, because once the deed was done and the swing bin lid had closed over the final square, there was a pause, and then his face screwed up and his eyes went shiny, and

'MUMMMEEEEE!'

Mummmeeeee arrived, comforted my brother, kept a straight

face long enough to tell me off and then – as she told me later – retired to another room so that she could laugh without our hearing. My brother was given another identical blanket and my mum had another story to add to the family canon of sibling lore: Auntie Marian cut our father's initials into the glass on the china cabinet with our grandmother's engagement ring! Lisa told Nikki she had to watch out for the Bunk Bed Monsters! Joanne cut up Julian's blanket – how adorably textbook! We laughed and we laughed.

*
**

My brother spent the middle year of his degree in the States, at the University of Massachusetts. I had finished mine by then and was living back with our parents, feeling stuck. But he had got away, properly launched himself. He was even going out with someone, a feat I had never managed in all my twenty-one years. It was all part of a broader, astonishing talent he had for doing normal things, like taking driving lessons, or going to music concerts, or drinking enough to actually get drunk. Astonishing to me at least, because it wasn't a talent I shared.

While he was at UMass, he even took part in a drugs trial.

'What sort of drug?' I asked. We were having one of our long, transatlantic phone calls; he was in his dorm and I was using the phone attached to the kitchen wall at home. I don't know why, because the phone in my parents' bedroom was much the better one for rambling conversations – it was more private and you could sit down to use it. The kitchen phone was for receiving news, taking messages and making arrangements. It wasn't a great phone to use for challenging or defending family narratives. I'm sure my brother didn't realize which phone I was on.

'A psychotropic one.'

'What did it do to you?'

'Nothing much – I just felt like I was floating above my bed for a bit. It was quite fun, actually. The researcher came round at the end and asked me a load of questions and when he asked if everything was normal now I said, "Yes, thanks, except for all the flying pink elephants" and he looked really scared for a moment.'

I could believe that: my brother had a way of deadpanning absurdities that could knock reality on its side for a second, before you realized what he was up to and had to try and pretend you knew all along.

'And then you told him you were joking.'

'Yes, obviously. But listen – before we started, they gave us this questionnaire to fill in, about our childhoods and so on. Did you know I could count as physically abused?'

'*What*? But we were hardly ever smacked.'

'I'm not talking about Mum and Dad, I'm talking about you – you were always hitting me.'

'But that was just normal sibling stuff – I know we used to fight, but...'

I left a moment for him to start laughing, but he didn't. He really wasn't joking.

'You used to hit me all the time when we were small. You used to hit me for no reason.'

All I could do was say sorry. I was in no position to deny that I used to hit him, because I remembered perfectly well that I had. One incident was even on tape. We were tiny – I was no more than three and my brother was still a toddler – and our father had just bought a tape recorder and a microphone. He gave me the microphone first and I sang 'Long-Haired Lover from Liverpool' into it. Then Dad took the microphone back and told me it was my brother's turn.

As my brother was too little to figure what to do by himself, Dad tried to get him to join in a game that they liked to play with him and had also played with me when I was first learning to speak: they would start a line of a nursery rhyme, then stop before the end and wait for the child to say the last word.

The tape is long lost, but I remember how it went:

Dad: 'Twinkle twinkle, little—'

My brother: 'No!'

Dad: 'How I wonder what you—'

My brother: 'No!'

Dad: 'Up above the world so—'

My brother: 'NO!'

At this point there is a dull thump, and my brother starts crying.

Dad: 'Joanne! What did you do that for? Ruth! Joanne's hit Julian! What should I do?'

∗∗

I know we used to fight, but…

… much of the time we only threw words at each other, and silly ones at that. I would shout *Moonface!* or *Nesthead!* and Julian would respond with *Mrs P.!* The origins of my chosen insults were obvious, but I never knew what 'Mrs P.' meant. It turned out that Julian didn't either, but he knew that for some reason it would never fail to hit its mark, so he kept throwing it.

I know we used to fight but…

… often it was only play-fighting. Sometimes we would put on our Mothercare dressing gowns and bow before we started, because that meant we were both Hong Kong Phooey.

∗∗

During my first term at university in Cambridge my brother came to pay a visit by himself. He sat down on the edge of my bed and looked round my college room, still bare but for a few books and cassettes, and one lonely-looking poster with a picture of a David Hockney narcissus on it.

I had realized from seeing other people's rooms that it was my job to decorate my own, and had only just bought and hung the poster. My brother dutifully admired it as I passed him a mug of coffee. I took my own mug and sat down on the desk chair, perching on the edge much as my brother was doing on the bed. Neither of us quite felt able to inhabit this space, let alone own it. Outside the family home, away from the family, we understood that it would make no sense to play our customary roles, but we were not sure yet how to talk to each other without resorting to the usual script.

Julian asked me how I was finding it here. Kind of weird, I said, and elaborated a little: about how difficult it was to organize my own work, about the boy I had a crush on, about the problems I was having fitting in to a social life which seemed to revolve around the bar, when I couldn't stand the taste of alcohol…

'But do you think you could be happy here?' he asked. 'Do you think you at least have the potential to be happier than you were at home?'

'I hoped I would be,' I said, 'but actually I'm quite depressed.' Julian sighed.

'What? Do I have to be happy? Is it compulsory?'

'It's just that… when you were at home, your problems filled the whole house.'

*⁎

For the first few months after we return from Plainsville, I pick up the phone every Sunday to dial the number that used to be my brother's, his widow answers, and then we talk for half an hour – well, mostly, she talks and I listen; I am almost as cagey with her as I am with my mother, although for different reasons. She tells me how she is, which, understandably, is not at all good. She tells me how Giselle asked where her daddy was, and when told he was in the sky, said, 'I go plane.'

She tells me about the difficulties my brother was having at work, and about the trouble she is experiencing in his wake. She tells me how much my mother hurt him, and not only recently either, but way, way back.

'I felt so sorry for Julian. He told me that one day he came out of school, and someone had hit him, and he was covered in blood – and your mother just ignored it, she just carried on walking like nothing had happened.'

'Really? I don't remember Julian getting hit like that when he was small. He did get punched once at the bus station, but he was in the sixth form then. He came home by himself and burst into tears – he was ashamed, he didn't want me to tell Mum, but—'

'Maybe, but my therapist said that the vulnerability Julian had, that made him kill himself – it had to come from early trauma.'

'Early trauma like…? I'm sorry – I know I can't speak for Julian, but I honestly don't remember anything really terrible. And I can't imagine Mum ever ignoring blood – if anything, she fussed too much.'

'He said he tried to talk to you about your mother, but you always said she wasn't so bad… and the therapist said not to be hard on you, you had to live with her all the time, so of course you had to protect yourself.'

'You mean, the therapist said we were emotionally abused, but I couldn't afford to acknowledge it?'

'Exactly… Julian worried about you. I would say he should tell you how bad he was feeling, about his work and your mother, but he always said, "No – leave Joanne alone! She's happy with her family – and she's fragile!"'

'He thought I was fragile?'

'Yes. You remember that phone call – when you told him what your mum said at your first period? When he put the phone down, he cried so much – he was so angry and upset for you.'

'Oh dear. I wish I'd never told him that. It backfired. I'm sorry.'

'He kept saying "Joanne's fragile", but all the time he was the most fragile of all of us.'

'I wish I'd known. I'm sorry.'

And I say, once more, I'm sorry. I can say it again and again, I can utter it every moment for the rest of my life, but *sorry* cannot lighten the yoke of my transgressions.

∗∗

As my sister-in-law is still in no state to deal with us, we have now exhausted the hospitality of all the other faculty members and it is the chair's turn to take us out, tell us how talented he thought my brother was, treat us to another informal lecture about the town's history and principal features, and introduce us to another of its restaurants.

Everybody in the faculty knows who I am the minute they set eyes on me: I look like a short, female copy of the young professor who's just killed himself. By now I have become very accomplished at guessing who they might be, based on what their faces do next: students or postdocs from his lab look sorry and wistful; peers look sad but in a more contained way – adults controlling themselves in front of the children; superiors look nervous. The man at the bar is obviously a boss.

The chair of the faculty had that same look on his face when he shook my hand in his office a few days back. Now he is smiling as he leads Mum and me into the best restaurant in town, and here is his vice-chair waiting for us at the bar, almost visibly shaking.

The chair is a much better politician than his deputy – presumably that's how you get to be chair. The deputy is thin, bespectacled, a clichéd picture of a nervy academic, but the chair, I imagine, was once a great high-school athlete – John Updike's Rabbit Angstrom, but with more brains. He suggests what to order. He asks about my work, my husband, my son. He shows me pictures of his own children. He would no more relinquish control of a conversation than he would the ball.

In this way, he propels us through two courses without anyone crying or bolting or starting a fight. The dessert menu arrives.

'Oh, they have sticky toffee pudding!' I say.

'You like that?' Rabbit asks.

'Yes. I didn't expect to see it, it's just so – quintessentially English.'

'You should have it, then – go on! Have it!'

'I haven't got the room.'

'Then I'll have it!'

He orders the sticky toffee pudding. While we wait for it to arrive, we have the conversation about the university and the town: what we've seen of it so far, who's shown us round, where we've eaten, where we're staying, where we've shopped, how it all compares with other parts of the States, how it compares with home... And then the vice-chair asks, 'Did Julian ever indicate that he appreciated what Plainsville had to offer?'

Mum's and Rabbit's faces freeze; the vice-chair looks desperate. I want to say, 'Well, I think he voted with his feet, mate,' but instead I say that he never said anything either way – which is not true, but it will serve.

I assume that the worst moment of the evening has now passed, but then Rabbit's sticky toffee pudding arrives. He takes up a forkful and holds it out to me.

'I need you to test this for me,' he says, 'so I know it's the real thing.'

There is nothing I can do but take a mouthful of pudding from Rabbit's fork, and swallow. I've got to behave: nice girls don't spit.

*

My conversations with Ayako have given me many new painful images to add to my stock. The most persistent is the one of my brother as a small child – no more than six – trailing behind my mother – and, unavoidably, me – crying, bloody and ignored. As a picture of something that really happened, I just can't credit it: my mother didn't always pick up on distress, but she noticed tears, and she certainly noticed blood.

On the other hand, I feel that there must be a necessary truth embodied in that figure: the blood-stained child, ignored and weeping. Wherever I go, I sense him shuffling behind me, hiccupping with grief. If I imagine myself turning round to look him in the face, I am bombarded by memories of my brother's tears: the times he cried as a boy and it was my fault, because I'd hurt him, or belittled him, or ganged up on him with our cousin, or left him out; the times he cried and it wasn't my fault, because he'd hurt himself, or was constipated, or had chicken pox, or someone who wasn't me had been mean to him; the times he cried and it was just annoying, because, say, Dad had bought him a packet of Fruit Gums without realizing, telepathically, that Julian didn't like them any more...

And then I see the bigger, older Julians. My first thought when Ayako told me this story had been that she must be thinking of the bus-station incident that happened during his teens, when some stranger had picked on him because of his private-school uniform, followed him onto a bus shouting abuse, and then punched him in the face. No one on the bus had done or said anything. They had ignored him, or – worse – pretended to. They had surely let him down.

And what about us? A death like Julian's feels like an accusation. Mum, Ayako and I, we are all of us compelled to turn round and look at that crying boy; then we cannot help but look at each other, and we cannot pretend to ourselves that we are not being looked at. Without even meaning to, we magnify each other's guilt, compound each other's pain. Just before Christmas, I receive an email from Ayako, saying that, although she likes me and knows I mean well, she can't continue to talk to me as long as I feel I have to defend our mother. I'm sorry about this, but I'm far from surprised. My sister-in-law has enough to deal with without having to deal with us.

∴

Dream, April 2009

Julian and I are adults but also children and his death both has and hasn't happened. He is larking around with a gun which is either real or a toy, pointing it at his head and shouting, 'Aaaggh no! I'm gonna shoot myself!' Then he passes the gun to me and says, 'Now you do it!' I'm already crying and I shout, 'How could you, after what happened?' Julian puts his hand on my shoulder and says he's sorry.

∴

I don't want to write about ugly feelings and ugly encounters, to tell these stories that make nobody look good, but I must. So:

Since my brother died, I have come to resent my mother for living. I am filled with rage towards her – whether it properly belongs to me or to him or to both of us I can't say – and I have come to see the last eighteen months of my brother's and mother's relationship as a zero-sum game which has been won by the more single-minded, and therefore less worthy, competitor.

'I know it's awful,' I tell my therapist, 'but I keep wishing she was dead. I feel like a petulant teenager – I hate her just for being *her.*'

'When you were an actual teenager, were you angry then?

'Yes. Of course.'

'Did you ever tell her you wished she were dead?'

'No – I used to say that I wished I'd never been born, and once Mum said, "Well, if we'd known, we'd've sent you back!"'

I laugh. The therapist doesn't.

'But that's a different thing,' she says. 'I'm talking about telling her you wished *she* were dead. Did you never say that?'

'No.'

'Then do you realize that most teenagers do?'

I never said it then – it wouldn't have occurred to me to say it. Perhaps if I'd had the thought then, at the developmentally appropriate time, it wouldn't be tormenting me now, along with the other thought I never had as a teenager:

I would rather DIE than turn out like you! Not only do I want my mother dead, but I want to murder everything in me that reminds me of her. I want to wipe the family resemblance off my face. All my rage at what has happened to my brother and to our family has concentrated itself in her, the mother who phones me every day, who walks through my door once a week, who looks after my son, drives me, her non-driving daughter, to the post office, the supermarket, the garden centre – and today, the vet school, where our younger cat is about to have an operation on an injured leg.

I am upset, feeling sorry for the cat, worried about the cat, guilty about the injury, guilty about what she's about to go through. On the way back, Mum and I have an argument, our first, post-Julian.

It's Mum's birthday soon. She wants to celebrate it by taking me, Chris and our son to see Dora, Lisa's daughter, performing in *The Sound of Music* in the West End. But I don't want to go. I *really* don't want to go.

'Can't we just take you out to lunch here?' I ask. 'To the Plough, maybe. You like the Plough.'

'I don't want to have lunch here. I want you to come to London and see your cousin in the show. You haven't seen her yet – don't you want to?'

'It's not that I don't want to see her – I'm just not that keen on *The Sound of Music*, Chris hates musicals altogether, and I think the boy will just be bored. And if I've got to schlep him all the way—'

'It'll be *fine*. It'll be *exciting* for him to see his cousin.'

'Hmm.'

And then I think of another objection – a real, practical one, not just a stalling exercise.

'But where will we stay? You'll have sold the house by then.'

'I might already be in the new flat, and if I'm not, you can stay with me at Uncle Brian's. He won't mind.'

'Have you asked him?'

'You know I don't have to. It's *family*. Dora's *family*.'

'I know, but—'

'And it's my *birthday*.'

It's my BIRTHDAY. It's FAMILY. I can't explain why to her – it's too painful – but the very words my mother is using to make her case are the very words that are triggering my resistance. I'm thinking about all the stories Julian and Ayako have told me about her obsession with family birthdays, how if he forgot hers she would go on and on about it, even if he was ill, or busy, or stressed – and he was usually all three. How she had him drive her round Berkeley, when she visited him there, even though his back was bad and driving was agony, because she had decided that he should take her out to buy her a special parka for her trip to somewhere cold – the Antarctic or polar north, I can't remember which – to make up for the fact that – as she kept reminding him – he had FORGOTTEN HER BIRTHDAY.

As for FAMILY, it put me in mind of the one and only occasion Julian had travelled to the UK with Ayako, intending to introduce her to his friends in London, in France, in Spain, only to find that my mother had scheduled a full programme of family visits without consulting him first. The first was a Seder night at her house, with the extended family at its noisiest and my cousin's baby screaming all the way through. Ayako told me later that she had gone to the bathroom to cry.

I can't allude to any of this. Instead I say, 'It's just… it reminds me of growing up, when you were always dragging me out to things I hated – athletics competitions, *Crocodile Dundee*…'

'Oh yes, poor, poor you, you had such a *traumatic* upbringing.'

'There's nothing funny about our upbringing any more,' I snap. She apologizes, and at once I feel so terribly remorseful that I give in. She can have what she wants: FAMILY on her BIRTHDAY.

**

Sometime in the late 1940s, my mother had a particularly nasty and persistent cold, so my grandmother took her to see the doctor. The doctor was less interested in the cold than in the fact that my mother had a very noticeable twitch, something my grandmother hadn't thought worth mentioning. She (I always imagine this doctor as a 'she') referred my mother to a child psychotherapist at the Tavistock Clinic in Hampstead. The therapist asked my mother to draw pictures of herself and her family, which she did, and to recount her dreams. My mother could never remember her dreams, but she wanted to please the nice lady, so she made some up. She would always say as an adult that she thought the therapist must have known they were made-up dreams, but wouldn't have minded – they were grist to the therapeutic mill, either way.

**

Here are the white (English) roses, piled up in a vast and expensive-looking arrangement on a table in the middle of a university function room. Along with lesser flowers and tasteful bits of greenery, they have been formed into a snow-covered memorial mountain, with a buffet in its foothills. It looks as though somebody has gone to a great deal of trouble, so I force myself to eat a little. The cold meats are very good; the cheese is too. It occurs to me that Julian would have enjoyed it, and then I can't manage any more.

At the front of the hall there is a long table with drinks and an open book of condolence, but – as per our wishes – no photograph of the absent guest of honour. At the back of the hall there are throne-like wooden chairs for Mum and I to sit on. Ayako's is empty; she has said all along that she won't be able to face it, and she is as good as her word.

We resist our enthronement as long as we can, remaining in the shadow of the buffet mountain, where Kathy introduces Mum to a couple of other faculty wives, and I'm accosted by a tiny, fierce woman who works in a high school in a neighbouring city. Julian did some science outreach with her; he was great at it – she loved him, the kids loved him.

'And these are not the easiest kids, you know? They're not easy to engage, but he had a way of doing it.'

'I had no idea he was doing that kind of work. He never mentioned it.'

'Well, he was a natural. A great ambassador. You know, when I heard, I was in the car and I got a phone call. I couldn't believe it, I just pulled the car over and I phoned my own brother. I just had to hear his voice…' She takes hold of my arm. 'What this must have done to you – you have every right to be mad at him. You cuss him, you cuss him good!'

'I will,' I say. 'Oh, believe me, I will – and thank you.'

'No, thank *you*. He was a great guy, you can be proud of him – and cuss him too.'

Lindsey appears and puts her hand on my shoulder; it's time for the thrones. Mum and I move reluctantly to the back of the hall, and people start lining up. I'm not new to this; I've been to funerals, including my own father's, when I was in the receiving line, but on that occasion I recognized most of the mourners who filed past – who hugged me, or took my shoulders or shook my hand, according to how well we knew each other – and even those I didn't know came from a context that meant something to me: Dad's work, or his grammar school or, in one case, his National Service years. This is quite different. With Ayako absent, the mourners have only two women they've never met to file past, and if Mum and I recognize someone, it's only because we've met them in the past week. We have no part of my brother in common. It could hardly be more awkward, and it can't be satisfying for anybody.

The chair, Rabbit Angstrom, is here. He shakes my hand very firmly and says, again, what a brilliant scientist he thought my brother was. All the faculty members – and there are quite a few of them by now – who have taken us out to lunch or dinner reiterate their condolences, and ask how we're holding up.

A tearful group of women whose children attend the same nursery as Giselle promise us that they'll take care of her. We apologize for Ayako; they had to bring this forward while we were here, we say; it's just too soon for her, we add. And it's true. We came here with some vague idea that we might be able to help, but in truth we've only made it worse.

An elderly man comes over and introduces himself as an emeritus professor at the faculty.

'It was quite a shock when I heard about Julian. Was he depressed?'

'I don't know… it would appear so.'

'That is strange – he seemed perfectly cheerful the last time I saw him.'

At this point he changes subject and spends a good five minutes telling me why he has dedicated his retirement to proving that all of Shakespeare's works were written by the Earl of Oxford.

After he has moved away, Lindsey sidles over discreetly and asks if I'm OK.

'I hope he didn't say anything to upset you.'

'Oh no,' I say. 'It was just – different.'

'I'm glad you're not upset. They're all chemists here – emotional intelligence is not really their forte.'

'I get that.'

Someone else is waiting to talk to me, an older woman wearing a gingham dress trimmed with lace, as if she has come fresh from the hoedown. I stand up to greet her and she hugs me, bruisingly hard. Then she takes me by the shoulders and tells me that my FAITH will see me through. It won't, but I thank her anyway.

Later, as the last of the company is draining out of the hall, I wait for Mum by the door. Kathy is with me, and Jessica, one of Julian's colleagues.

'This really is a great turnout,' she tells me. 'I hope you can find some comfort in it. It shows the impact Julian had – we didn't get so many when Craig Venter spoke.'

I've been too appropriate for too long, and now I break: 'And they say it's only a career move for poets.'

Jessica does laugh, but Kathy's smile freezes. 'Ooh, that's warped.'

Of course it's warped. Everything's warped – and Julian, incidentally, would've laughed his fucking head off.

*
**

What's purple and lives at the bottom of the ocean?

Moby Plum.

Mum said she never understood why this made the two of us crease up so much. But it did, to the extent that when I went to a Jackson Pollock retrospective with Chris and a wide field of purple in one of his paintings reminded me of the joke, I repeated it aloud and then promptly collapsed into giggles. We were in the middle of a gallery, and no one else was laughing. My husband was amused, but utterly bewildered.

Julian and I both suffered terribly from inappropriate, uncontrollable fits of giggles. They could be brought on out of nowhere by the imagining or recollection of funny things, inevitably something that could never be explained properly to anyone else who happened to be around. We'd both had the experience, in school, of having to pretend to have coughing fits in order to cover up the fact that we were laughing for no apparent reason in an echoey corridor. I got so good at this that people would rush up and ask if I was OK, if I needed to sit down, or maybe have a drink of water?

I would like to think that, if I'd gone first, he would have remembered something silly at my funeral. And pretended to cough.

*
**

'Mum said we were in this together,' I tell my therapist, 'and I said, "No, we're in this separately." I know I'm being unkind, but I just want her to understand: we're not mourning the same person, we don't have the same story. I feel I've got to defend myself – it's like she'll *absorb* me if I don't.'

'I've said before, haven't I, that the three of you were too enmeshed?'

'Yes. My brother's way of cutting himself free was a little drastic, though, wasn't it?'

'It was.'

'I can't stay in the same room as Mum. I feel like her grief's taking up all the room. And she cries really easily – it's on a hair trigger. But then I… especially when she's around, I can hardly squeeze out a tear… I'm so angry with her, I don't even know whose anger it is, mine or Julian's. I think it might be his…'

'Do you feel close to him when you feel his anger?'

'Yes. I'm keeping him here. He's still here… but we hadn't talked properly for ages… I wish he'd talked to me. I'm angry with him too.'

'For leaving you?'

'Yes, but also for not talking to me before – shutting me out. And who said he could bagsy suicide, anyway? I don't remember agreeing to that. *I* was always the depressed one. The clever, depressed one. I always thought I'd get a first, get a PhD, and then kill myself – and then he did… I mean, I know I'm being flippant—'

'But you're not.'

'I mean, it's not as if I didn't know what it was like to feel dark and empty. He *knew* I knew, he *knew* I understood, I could have talked him through it… I understand how he felt, I think, I just don't understand why he acted on it. Why did he *do* that?'

'Maybe the darkness was just too dark and the emptiness was too empty.'

I've been bulldozing through the session, with my anger and my resentments, but this stops me short.

'The truth is,' my therapist continues, 'that you've had a parting of the ways: you're still here in the world, and he isn't, and it's *unbearable*.'

I find I am suddenly able to cry.

*⁎

Sometimes people say, 'You should try and live a happy life. He wouldn't have wanted you to be sad.'

Forgive me if I beg to differ.

*⁎

It would be better if my anger could be contained within my therapist's outdoor consulting room, if I could only leave it there and visit it once a fortnight, but it resists any kind of containment. It skulks all over the house I share with two quite innocent people. Chris says:

'Look, Joanne, I know you're hurting, but you've been very hostile to me lately, I don't like it and I've done nothing to deserve it.'

*⁎

November 2009. My son has started going to after-school club on Fridays. He has company, and I have a longer working day.

That's the theory, anyway, but in practice I spend the extra two hours wandering about the house, finding it too quiet, missing him. Today I have been even more distractible than usual, so I give up any pretence of working and go to pick him up early.

I mean it to be a nice surprise, but I interrupt him in the middle of his turn on the PlayStation. He has been waiting for this for twenty minutes – an age to a six-year-old, and he is furious.

'I hate you,' he hisses, as we walk home. 'I hate you so much I could kill you. I want to cut you up into such tiny pieces that ants can carry you.'

When we get home he switches on the TV and I make supper and then he doesn't hate me any more.

∴

Dream, January 2011

Mum and I are ready to leave America now. We are part of some kind of touring party, sitting in a glassed-off waiting room at the airport, off the main concourse. I tell our guide I need the toilet. Before I go through the sliding glass doors on the main concourse, she hands me a pair of yellow-tinted eye protectors, which she takes from a tray by the door.

'Put these on', she says, 'the glare is terrible – it leads to a lot of violence. You need to turn left at the Office of Suicides.'

Just as I am leaving, a man from our party approaches the guide and starts to complain to her about the tough regulations at the airport, the way they use thought control. Then he bends down to pick up a paperback from the ground, a dystopian novel from the fifties, and as he does so, the guide shoots him, point-blank, no warning, and then without missing a beat turns back to me, smiling.

Outside the waiting room I see a sign:

Pill for Joanne Limburg

Please take this as you may have been disturbed or distressed
by what happened.

This will help.

I take the white pill and after that I can't seem to stop smiling.

The way into the toilet is confusing; there are two doors,
both at the far end of a wiggling maze of paths and turnstiles.
Depending on how well I find my way through I will wind up
either through the right-hand door, to the toilets, or through the
left-hand door which leads to a white porcelain and chrome
chamber which supposedly houses a breath-cleaning service,
but is really an evil place where they strip out people's lungs
in order to sell them; at the back, they have three baths set into
the ground which are filled with white lung broth, next to a sign
that says

Drink a pint of lung.

I manage to get through the right-hand door but as I do I see
that a friend from home has gone through the left – I realize this
is because I cheated at the last minute to get through the right,
and I feel guilt-stricken and guilty. But there is nothing I can do
now. If I am going to be allowed to use a toilet I will have to pass
an inspection. To do this I have to climb into a dry bath naked
with a naked old man who inspects my genitals. He pinches both

nipples, touches me far more than is necessary and then passes me 'Clean'.

When I rejoin the group it is time to move on the next stage. We are driven across the airport site in a coach, past buildings I am reassured to see look more British than American. Soon we are at passport control and customs, so very nearly on the plane and home, but as the queue moves and I approach the desk, I become terrified that they will find something illegal in my luggage that will give them an excuse to detain me here. Next to the line of people is a huge, messy pile of confiscated goods, and at the very top of it I see a copy of an anthology that has a poem of mine in it. The name of the book is *Staying Alive*.

⁎

My therapist says:

'I'll tell you what I'm thinking – you may not like it, but when I hear you talking about how you feel responsible for your brother's death, it reminds me of how sometimes small children, when one of their parents is ill, or their parents are splitting up, think it must be their fault somehow, and they think this partly because they are still quite solipsistic at that age, and can't quite conceive of something that has nothing to do with them, but also because if it's their fault, then they're still in control, they can understand it. You see, the idea that it might have nothing to do with them is just so much scarier. It's not that I think you're always like a five-year-old child – I'm not judging you like that

– but I believe there will be something about this particular kind of magical thinking that will ring bells with you, in the situation you've found yourself in – does that make sense? Am I being fair here?'

Vessel Six

Q: What is the Jewish attitude to cremation?

A: *Jewish law forbids the mutilation of corpses. Traditionally,
cremation is regarded as such. However, more progressive
Jewish communities will now accept cremation.*

*
**

A few months after Julian's death, my mother puts the family
home on the market and starts hunting for a new place to live – a
flat or maisonette, somewhere smaller, and nearer to her friends.
She couldn't take everything with her, even if she wanted to.
There has to be a clear-out and I have to help her with it, but first
I have some ashes to scatter.

*
**

On our last evening in Plainsville I meet Kathy in the hotel lobby,
to thank her once more, and to take delivery of half my brother's
ashes.

She hands me a stiff, square paper bag with twisted paper
handles. It's black, with the name of the funeral home on it in silver

lettering, and it looks as if it should hold something expensive and luxurious in it – a raw silk evening dress, a Prada bag – instead of what it does contain, which is both priceless and abject.

Priceless, abject and surprisingly heavy. Is this really only part of him? He wasn't tall, only tall-ish, and not what you'd call a big man.

'Thank you for this,' I say, 'and for everything else you've done for us.'

'Not at all. It's been a pleasure to meet you both.'

'I hope it's not been too difficult for you…'

'It's been no trouble at all.'

'Mum said to say goodbye, and thank you. She's having a rest…'

'That's fine, I understand. She must be exhausted.'

'She is. It's been… very hard for her.'

'And for you too. You'll be glad to get back to your family.'

'Yes, I certainly will.'

I say goodbye to Kathy and her smile, and then I carry the half-Julian up to my room, where I put it down on the unused twin bed. I peer into the top of the boutique bag and see only another bag, a plastic carrier. Inside the carrier bag is a matter-of-fact, unceremonious lidded cardboard box with my brother's name on the side. I lift the box, and as I do I feel the weight of its contents shift about, like sand in a bucket. I can't look. I put the box back in the plastic carrier, and the plastic carrier back in the stiff, black paper.

That night, as I've done so many times on family holidays, I share a twin room with my brother.

∗∗

We shared all kinds of spaces: twin rooms, dens beaten out of the long grass, the hollow underneath the greengage tree in our back garden, and an old iron cot in our grandparents' box room. It made the perfect Tardis.

Our Doctor Who was Tom Baker. Every Saturday evening my cousins, my brother and I would watch him battle Daleks, Cybermen and Silurians on the TV set in our grandparents' front room, while we sat wide-eyed in front of it, eating cold beef sandwiches and Mr Kipling's French Fancies.

It wasn't enough to watch. We wanted to travel with the Doctor. For that, we had the cot in the box room. For anyone else, it would have remained just a cot, but as my cousin Nikki, Julian and I were secretly Doctor Who's children, we were able to adapt it for travel through time and space. For some reason, I decided that the name of the game was not 'Doctor Who's Children' but 'The Children of the Wind' – I must have liked the sound of it.

∗∗

And now half my brother's ashes and I are on a train to London, sharing a double seat. Though to call them 'ashes' is more polite than accurate. I know because I've done my research. I wanted to find out exactly what happened to my brother's body, to take the journey with him so that, in my imagination at least, he wouldn't be going through death alone. For that reason, I have been reading up on cremation. I know that the body was placed in a container – not a coffin, but something more basic and functional. This container was inserted ('charged') into an insulated chamber (the 'retort'), where it and its contents were burnt at a temperature which might have been as low as 760°C or as high as 1150. After two hours of this, my brother's organs and soft tissue – the intestines that hurt when he was a little boy, the back muscles that pained him as an adult, the heart he chose in the end to starve of oxygen – had all been turned to gas and discharged into the Plainsville sky. Only the bones remained. It would have taken about twenty minutes to grind them down into the lumpy grey-and-white sand I have in the holdall on the next seat.

So, to put it accurately: half of my brother's ground bones and I are on a train to London, sharing a double seat. It is a Saturday in November. We are going to our soon-to-be-gone family home, where we will meet my brother's oldest and closest friends, then the three-and-a-bag of us will head out together, ready for the scattering.

*
*

We have our last Midwestern breakfast at the home of John and Ellen, a pair of emeritus professors. They inhabit a lushly green space just outside town, much visited by the local wildlife; on the way here, Ellen had to brake sharply to avoid running over a wild turkey that had chosen that moment to hurl itself across the road.

'You see so many of them,' she said. 'What a lot of people don't realize is that Benjamin Franklin actually thought the turkey should be the official emblem of the United States, not the eagle. Imagine that!'

'You might have wound up with a very different sort of nation,' I said.

'Quite,' she said. 'Different indeed.'

And talking of counterfactual histories, how might it have turned out for Julian if he had only told John and Ellen how much he was struggling? The subject comes up, inevitably, during our breakfast.

'We knew something was up,' Ellen says, pouring coffee, 'but he kept so much to himself. We had no idea, if we'd only…'

'And we could have been in a position to help,' says John. 'We're effectively independent of the faculty now, but we still have influence.'

I tell them as much as I've been told.

'I just don't get it,' John says. 'He was such a gifted scientist – the work he was doing, it was really exciting – and he'd just brought in that grant, that million-dollar grant… I wish he'd felt able to speak to us.'

'He wasn't talking to anyone,' Mum says. 'He just isolated himself more and more. I knew something was wrong – I kept checking his web page again and again, just to see he was still working, still there.'

And my mother's instincts were right after all. I thought he only needed some space from us. I thought he'd come back. I was wrong.

We manage, somehow, to turn the conversation round, and now John is asking me about my writing. He's googled me; very impressive, he says. I try to answer his questions but I'm having trouble concentrating, not just because of the grief, but also because of the noise – someone has been using a buzz saw nearby, and it's been getting louder and louder and louder. Now it feels as if it's taking the top of my head off.

'I'm sorry,' I say at last. 'I'm a bit distracted by your neighbour.'

'Our neighbour? What do you mean?'

'That saw – are they having some work done?'

'That saw?'

'Yes, there it goes again – just there!'

They stop and listen, and then laugh.

'Oh, that's not a saw. What you're hearing are the male dog-day cicadas – they're calling for the females! They do it every summer.'

'It's deafening!'

'Is it? It's just background noise to us – we're just used to it, I guess.'

That's background noise? God, this place! The humidity, the chiggers, the cicadas, the flat, endless distances, this ferocious sun

– it's a concerted assault. I come from a temperate little island, gently dampened with rain and irony. This is not my habitat. It was not Julian's, either. He was lost here: boiled, deafened and fatally landlocked.

Silently I blame this place, and my head fills again with angry noise that only I can hear.

***

My mother's house is at the tail end of Wemborough Road, and it really is a tail end, separated from the main, busier section by a traffic island with a 'keep left' sign on it. There are a handful of 1930s semis on our side of the tail, and a smaller number of l930s detached homes on the other. When the gardens and driveways have all dried up, the road bends sharply to the left and splits into three little cul-de-sacs, all postwar: Honister Gardens, Honister Close and Honister Place. Honister Place was a council estate – we were never allowed to ride our bicycles there.

Wemborough Road itself ends abruptly at a patch of wasteland we used to call 'the Green'. It has footpaths on either side, and rising up in the middle a long, unkempt plateau, covered in grass, cow parsley, nettles, dock leaves and other weeds I couldn't name; whatever they are called, they were always high enough to be beaten down into little clearings, perfect camp bases for our secret clubs. A muddy track down the centre leads to two trees, one ideal for communal climbing, the other accessible only to the oldest and tallest. If you climbed part way up the first tree you could see Wembley Stadium – we were proud of that.

∗∗

After the prayers at my mother's, Uncle Brian drives us back to Cambridge, and my cousin Nikki decides to come with us. We sit squashed up next to each other in the back seat, talking about Julian.

'I just keep remembering the three of us playing together at Nanny's,' she says. 'The three of us in that old cot, being "The Children of the Wind"…'

And we break off to laugh, because how could you not?

'I think I came up with that. I don't know what I was thinking of.'

'I don't know either… Anyway, I keep seeing the three of us, playing together in that cot, and everything was fine, and everything was normal, and we were all perfectly happy, but then I put that picture next to what's happened to Julian, and then I think, "Was it really ever that straightforward?"'

∗∗

We've packed up and checked out. We've said goodbye to Ayako. John and Ellen have driven us to the airport, where I snapped at Mum in front of them, and felt awful about it. Mum has cried again at the check-in desk, and I have allowed the security staff to put Julian's ashes through the scanner, along with the new shoulder bag I bought on one of our downtown shopping trips. We didn't come to Plainsville to shop, but it passed the time, and it seemed to reassure our hosts, to see that we liked this or that little piece of their town enough to pay for it and take it back home. So although we have come home without retrieving Julian, consoling his widow or attending any funeral, we have managed to gather a few new second-hand memories, we have our bits of shopping, and I have my black bag from the funeral home.

Mum didn't want to take the ashes away. When Kathy told us about Ayako's offer of half the cremains, she said no without thinking; Jews don't cremate, therefore we can't possibly want any ashes. It was an unpleasant surprise to her that she hadn't spoken for both of us. I explained that I was taking them for Julian's friends at home, so that they could say goodbye. This is a truth, but only a partial one. I am a big sister still, and I need to take care of my brother in my own way.

There are no special arrangements or permissions needed for transporting cremains. The security staff are not in the least bit fazed by them, and neither is the steward on the night flight from Chicago, who simply takes the bag from my hands and shoves it, with great good cheer, into the overhead locker.

I spend the flight wide awake and feeling sick. I feel as if I can't breathe on this plane. I want at every moment to get off it, but my brother took the only parachute.

⁂

One afternoon during the summer term of 1977, my brother's first at primary school, I was sitting cross-legged with the rest of my class on the carpet at the back of our Portakabin, while the deputy head told us a story.

'This is about a family of dragons,' she said, 'and they were all identical. Does anyone know what "identical" means?'

I put my hand up.

'Yes, Joanne.'

'Does it mean there were a lot of them?'

'No, that's not what it means.' And then she added: 'Your little brother knew.'

I felt humiliated, of course, but also betrayed. My mother, I realized, had been teaching my brother WORDS behind my back. I pictured them in a whispering huddle, sharing the treasure, keeping me out.

⁂

Mum says she doesn't feel able to come up with us. I'd never expected her to, but I don't say so.

'I thought we'd go to the trees in the middle,' I say, 'and do it round there.'

'They'll be able to see you from Belmont Synagogue there, won't they?' Mum asks. 'I wonder what the security guys will think you're up to.'

'I don't know, Mum, but I don't think it matters.'

The three of us – Paul, Elliott and I – decide to get the business out of the way as soon as possible. They have been Julian's friends since secondary school, so they weren't with him during our Green days, and as we walk along the track I tell them about our secret clubs, how we used to ride our bicycles along this very track, get up as much speed as possible, then lift our legs and practically fly down the slope at the end.

'I had a big row with Julian once, just over there' – I point down and to the right, to the paved footpath. 'We were… six and four, five and seven, something like that. I was trying to go one way on my bicycle, and he was trying to go the other way on his, but there was only room for one of us. In the end he pushed me and I fell into the nettles.'

'So he won, then,' says Paul.

'Yes, that time – but I wasn't exactly angelic to him… I did all sorts, I tied him up with green garden twine, I whacked him on the side with my violin case and bruised his hip… all sorts…'

'Everyone does all sorts to their siblings.'

'True… Anyway, here we are. I thought – if that's OK with you – that we could scatter the ashes round here, and it might be nice to share memories of Julian while we're doing it?'

I open the holdall, take out the cardboard box, open that, take out the clear plastic bag.

'Are you OK?' I ask. 'Are you both OK to do this?'

They are. I put my hand in, take out the first fistful, throw it. Only the heavier fragments fall to the ground; the finer grains spread out into a tiny dust cloud, and some settle back over me.

'All the neighbourhood kids came here,' I said. 'We were great tree climbers. We left our bicycles at the bottom, by the trunk.'

I hold the bag out and Elliott puts his hand in.

'I've realized this is the last time I'll ever touch him,' he says.

Paul takes his first fistful. From then on we take turns, throwing dust and telling stories. We are remembering three different relationships: Elliott and Julian shared confidences; Paul and Julian shared jokes.

'I only really got to know Julian in the sixth form,' Paul says. 'He was recovering from appendicitis and I had a broken leg, so we spent PE lessons playing cards. Julian invented these card games: there was "Repok" – that was like poker, except that you could only see your opponent's hand and not your own – and then there was "Pans", which was like Snap but with the cards played face down – and instead of shouting "Snap" or "Pans" you shouted "Olly-olly-ockenheimer".'

'I didn't know about any of this,' I say. 'We had our own jokes, though… like the Marmite Face. It's this…' I open my mouth wide and draw my lips over my teeth. 'It's what happens when you get Marmite between your lip and your gum.'

Paul says: 'We had this long-running joke that I only shat once a year – no idea when that came about, but whenever we were on the phone and he asked me how I was, I had to say, "Oh, you know – backed up."'

I say I felt at the end that he lost his sense of humour. Paul says not.

'The very last email he sent to me was... well, I've had this beard for a while, and I sent him a picture of my three-year-old daughter – who's obviously my daughter – and he just sent back this one line: "You look a lot younger without your beard."'

We've got to the bottom of the clear bag. We pat the dust off our own and each other's coats and turn back. I stop and look, for one last time, at the Climbing Tree.

'There's one memory that keeps coming back to me,' I say, 'and that's the time when Julian was six or seven, and he was hanging by his hands from that branch just up there, and he was panicking, kicking his legs about, and going "Help, I'm losing my grip!" again and again – and I was just laughing. I feel terrible now that I laughed.'

'You shouldn't torture yourself about it,' says Elliott. 'It's just one of those insignificant little things – it only seems meaningful now because of what's happened, but it doesn't have to be.'

'I know, but—'

'It was just a stupid little moment. You don't have to make it stand for everything.'

**

Julian and I always enjoyed being silly together. Most of all, we enjoyed being silly to music. It was an excellent way to fill time in the long summer holidays if we could find no one else to play with us. All we needed was a source of music, the chairs and the sofa to jump off and the living-room carpet to throw ourselves about on. We had a favourite cassette tape, *Chart-Busting Instrumental Hits*, which had come free with the milk one morning. It had 'Popcorn', for bouncing around to, and 'Sleepy Shores', good for Kate Bush impressions. We also liked to switch the television on in the mornings, when there was nothing on but 'Pages from Ceefax', and create, hilariously we thought, to the Ceefax music.

We both had vinyl record players, small ones that we could listen to in our rooms. This meant that when one of us liked a record and the other one didn't – for example, during that summer when Julian insisted on playing 'Flash' by Queen again and again and none of the rest of us could stand it – we could avoid fights. But quite often our tastes coincided, and then we would listen together on the stereo in the living room. Sometimes we would make 'radio programmes' with the cassette recorder, introducing our favourite records and then holding the microphone to the stereo speakers while we played them.

I can still remember some of the records we played into the microphone: 'Knowing Me, Knowing You' ('Ah-haaaaaa') by ABBA; 'Way Down' by Elvis Presley, which was the first single I'd ever bought with my own money; 'The Theme from M*A*S*H*' ('Suicide is painless'). The record we must have played more than any other, because we both loved it so much, was the Ian Dury and the Blockheads song, 'Hit Me with Your Rhythm Stick'. On one of the tapes we made, you could hear us shouting along to our favourite line, because it was something of a shared philosophy: 'IT'S NICE TO BE A LUNATIC!'

.:.

On the Tube into London, after the scattering, I share a joke with Paul and Elliott, one of the many that I'd heard from Julian first. The memorial joke goes as follows:

So there are these two guys drinking at the top of the Empire State Building. A third guy comes to join them and they get talking. They swap taller and taller tales, make bigger and bigger boasts, until one of the first two guys leans over to their new friend and says, 'Let me tell you a secret, buddy – the biggest, the one nobody wants you to know – but first of all, watch this.'

'Oh no, come on,' the other one says. 'Please, not this again – you promised—'

But his friend isn't listening to him. He gets up, climbs onto the parapet, launches himself off, flies once round the perimeter of the building, then lands safely on the roof again.

The third guy is, of course, astonished.

'Oh wow, that's amazing! That's the most incredible thing I've ever… You can… you can actually FLY!'

'I can. And that's not all… You see… you see, the truth is, I can fly, and you can fly, and he can fly – everybody can fly, and that's what they don't want you to know. So why don't—'

'No, not that,' his friend says. 'Stop it.'

'Shaddup! So you want a go?'

'Me? Now?'

'Sure. You saw me do it. You can too. All you need is confidence. Go on! Go ahead!'

So, with the encouragement of one of his new friends, and deaf to the pleadings of the other, the drunk man climbs up to the parapet, spreads his arms wide, leaps off...

... and drops like a stone.

Now the cautious guy shakes his head at the flying guy, who says, 'What?'

And his friend says, 'You're a cunt when you're pissed, Superman.'

**

One of the aunts who plagued our mother when she was growing up was her mother's youngest sister, Yetta. She was unmarried, intelligent, strong-willed, whip-tongued and entirely lacking in sensitivity. My mother told me that she had once come home to find that Yetta had gone through her things and was reading a letter from a university boyfriend.

'She didn't see that I had any right to be angry,' she said. 'I was her sister's daughter and she thought it was her business to know everything I did.'

Yetta continued to think that my mother's affairs were her business, and, especially after our grandmother died, that meant Julian and me. Were we healthy? Were we eating properly? Standing up straight? Doing the right things? With the right sort and number of friends? I say 'number' quite specifically: one of her many charges against me was that I only had two.

She treated the pair of us equally, up to a point. We both had birthday and Chanukah presents. We were both expected to give her good accounts of ourselves. We were each summoned to the phone before we began university for a dose of advice on how to comport ourselves away from home. But we were not equal entirely: as a girl, I was more firmly inside her jurisdiction, particularly when it came to my clothes, my manners and my general appearance. Also, I exasperated her in ways that my brother didn't. She couldn't put her finger on what it was about me, but...

'You,' she said one day, pointing to my brother, 'you're all right, I don't worry so much about you, but you,' and now she pointed to me, 'you're FUNNY.'

My brother and I excused ourselves as soon as we could, then ran upstairs together to let the inappropriate giggles out.

It occurs to me now that 'funny' must have had a very specific meaning in my mother's family. My uncle used it about my brother, after he died the way he did.

∗∗

There is a rosebush in our back garden that blooms in late May and early June, throwing out short-lived relays of delicate, sun-yellow flowers. We planted it in the summer of 2002, after I miscarried our first child, at the suggestion of a kind nurse I met on the gynaecology ward, who said she had done the same in memory of her own lost baby. We call it the 'Alex' rose; we had meant to name that child 'Alex' or 'Alix' after my grandfather, but after s/he was lost we agreed that we could never use the name again.

It is the first May since Julian's death, the month that has his first missed birthday in it. I still have some vestiges of him in the plastic bag which held his ashes, and I feel that now is the time to let them go, so I take the bag outside, turn it inside out over the Alex rose and give it a good shake. The last flakes of ash and bonemeal flutter down onto the flowerbed. He's with us here. He's gone.

Vessel Seven

Q: What should be done with prayer books and other holy objects, such as prayer shawls, when they are no longer used?

A: *The rabbi might begin with a text from Deuteronomy:*

12: 2–4: You must destroy all the sites at which the nations you are to dispossess worshipped their gods, whether on lofty mountains and on hills or under any luxuriant tree. Tear down their altars, smash their pillars, put their sacred posts to the fire, and cut down the images of their gods, obliterating their name from that site. Do not do the same thing to Adonai your God.

⁂

The rabbis responsible for the Talmud, that vast body of Jewish literature which interprets biblical law for everyday use, understood this phrase, Do not do the same thing to Adonai your God, as an absolute prohibition on erasing or destroying any transcription of the seven biblical names for God. Along with the Tetragrammaton Yod/Heh/Vav/Heh, these include: Adonai, El, Eloah, Elohim, Shaddai and Tzeva'ot. As these words represent God, so they partake of his holiness and must not be destroyed. They must be buried, like people, in consecrated ground, with proper ceremony and all due respect, for they have had life in them.

As it would be impractical to stage a separate burial for each item, every synagogue has a dedicated space known as a *genizah* (meaning 'reserved' or 'hidden') where used Torah scrolls, prayer books, old prayer shawls and phylacteries and other ritual objects are stored. If the rabbi or his congregation interpret the prohibition as extending to any appearance of one of the Hebrew names of God in any text, or even to any text in which the Hebrew name of God might appear, then other documents will join the scrolls: marriage contracts, business contracts, letters and so on.

There was once a community in medieval Cairo which adhered to this strict interpretation. Over the years, they filled a whole room with pieces of parchment and then abandoned it. Centuries later this cache was discovered by a Cambridge academic called Solomon Schechter, who shipped it to the University Library. I once visited it there. I was shown into a room where teams of conservators were restoring tiny scraps of parchment covered sometimes with prayers but more often with complaints, petitions, invoices, congratulations, condolences or tenancy agreements. One of the staff explained how much grime could accumulate on one scrap, and how long, how carefully, she had to work to remove it. She handed me a jar she kept on her desk. Feel the weight of that, she said – that's centuries of dust.

⁂

Mum is moving out of the house and into a smaller flat, so I have come down to London to help her decide what to keep and what to abandon. I have helped to clear out family homes before, but those were used homes, homes of the deceased.

Grandma – my mother's mother – died when I was seven. I went to the house with Mum. I remember feeling excited but also afraid – what if Grandma's ghost were there? There were no ghosts, but all the things that belonged to the house remained in their places. They were no less familiar for the absence of their owner. The red front door was there, and the telephone table, with the blue-and-white Joint Israel Appeal collection box sitting on it. The rubber plant was still in the living room, and the electric fire which had once felt too hot on my face because I had mumps; the china cabinet was there, and the wooden clock still ticked on top of it; the china birds were on the mantelpiece, along with the pink stone egg in its gold-coloured holder. The sideboard was still in the dining room, with a drawer full of rubber balls and pencils, and so was the biscuit barrel in the shape of a watermill. The larder and kitchen still smelled of salad cream.

Grandma's bedroom was less familiar to me, the wardrobe and drawers disgorging strange treasures as Mum went through them. I found a metal box with a picture of the Three Wise Monkeys on the lid. It was lined in red plush and filled with brooches – some ceramic and floral, others with bright paste stones. When we took it home, Mum let me keep it in my room. She shouldn't have:

I buried it under the greengage tree in the back garden, so that one day I could have the pleasure of finding it again, but although I tried many times, I never did.

∴

Julian and I were each allowed to choose a nicknack to take from Grandma's house. I chose the pink stone egg from the living room, and Julian chose the china watermill biscuit barrel. They were both placed on the windowsill in our dining room, alongside the Caithness glass paperweight and blue vase that made our voices go all low and funny when we sang into it. I have forgotten what – if anything – was kept in the barrel while it lived there. What I can't forget is the day that I pulled the lid off so roughly that the whole barrel fell to the floor and shattered. Mum shouted at me; Julian stood behind her, crying. It didn't matter that it was an accident – what was gone was gone.

∴

My Uncle Richard liked to tell a story about his little sister, my mother. Their Auntie Elsie married a man called Mr G. – and always known as Mr G., because he was not a man you could ever call 'Uncle'. One day he offered my mother, then still at primary school, a much-prized silver half-crown.

'On condition,' he said, 'that you promise to spend it on fruit – not sweets or cake or anything else that isn't healthy.'

'In that case,' my mother said, 'you can keep it.'

'I always admired your mum for that,' my uncle said. 'She could've lied and taken it but she wouldn't, she preferred to tell him what she thought of him. I don't think I'd ever've had the guts.'

That was always how my mother preferred to be seen: a woman with guts, a strong woman, a woman who was never afraid to tell men what she thought of them. It made her impatient when my uncle, after my brother's death and her diagnosis, would keep shaking his head and saying what a rotten life she'd had.

'I'd punch him,' she'd say, 'but right now I haven't got the strength.'

All the way through our childhoods, our teenage years, our earliest adulthood, this was the mother Julian and I knew: strong, competent, purposeful, someone who stepped in to sort out other's people's problems – she'd made a career of it, after all. We supposed, with the rest of the family, that it was she who propped our poor father up, not the other way round. But then he died, and three weeks later she was made redundant without warning. The strong shell ruptured, and my brother and I met the far more vulnerable woman who'd been living inside. She would eventually pick up the pieces, tack them together, and put them on to show to the world again, but Julian and I – and Julian especially, because he was the man now – would always be aware that this was our mother precariously mended, and never to be whole to us again.

Or as my brother put it when he came home for Dad's funeral: 'So that's our childhood over, then.'

⁂

Mum and I begin with the shelf at the top of her wardrobe.
A good third of it is taken up with wedding presents my parents
never liked or used, but which they had felt obliged to keep, for,
much as the written names of God partake of his holiness, so do
presents from relatives partake of their woundable feelings. Hence
my mother has held onto the mauve rayon damask tablecloth and
the floral china egg-coddlers, unused, since 1967. It is now 2008,
and the objects have long since outlived their donors. Finally, they
can go. Maybe someone will see them in a charity shop and find
them charmingly retro, and then they'll be loved and used at last.

Then there's my grandmother's good cutlery, salvaged thirty
years ago from the sideboard with the ball-and-pencil drawer.
Mum has never used it since she took it home, but when she did it
was because she remembered its being used, remembered setting
out the soup spoons and fish knives on the table on Shabbat,
remembered how later in the evening her mother would hand
them to her dripping wet, ready for her to wipe dry and put away.
They were the good spoons and knives – they deserved respect.

So they have spent the last thirty years in honourable retirement
at the top of my parents' wardrobe. They have gathered dust up
there. They have tarnished. The spoons and knives spread out on
my mother's duvet are not the spoons and knives she cleaned.
Not any more. Time for them to go.

⁂

Ayako has told me so many unhappy stories about my brother, how his confidence was kicked from under him, how he cried every night during his last months, how sometimes she found it hard to be patient with him and how dreadful she feels about that now, how he looked forward to our mother's visits but was always in pieces by the end of them, how he always knew he was the least important member of the family, and that was why he had the smallest room...

**

This last story is a shock to me. How could he let Ayako think that? How could he think that himself? His room might be small but it was built especially for him. When we were nine and seven, our parents took us away for a two-week holiday to Crete (where we ate the forbidden sandwiches), and when we came back the garage was missing, the wall between the dining room and living room had been knocked through, and there was a new, concrete-floored, windowless room at the back of the kitchen. The garage was going to be rebuilt, with my brother's room on top. He could move out of the tiny third bedroom and have his own proper space.

The new room was a separate realm. We lived in a typical 1930s suburban semi, with the staircase on the left and the landing on the right. The staircase ended in a big, square tread with a small step up to the landing, and nothing to the left but a frosted window with a little pane of green-and-yellow stained glass and a small sill underneath. Before the building work, you could only turn right; after the building work, you could choose to turn left instead. Left was Julian's room. My brother had his very own direction.

*
**

'Is there any point in keeping any of Julian's old stuff?' my mother asks. 'I guess we should just throw it out...?'

'Really?'

'He won't be coming back for it, and I'll have no room for it. Do you want any of it?'

'I don't know, I'll have a look... I thought I might fill a box – for Giselle.'

'That's a nice idea. But you'll keep it in your house, won't you?'

'Till she's old enough. Yes.'

So I turn left. The room, though long enough, is narrow, and it's true that there isn't much space in it. It's like a truncated corridor, with a window at one end and the wardrobe at the other. The bed runs alongside one of the longer walls with its headboard underneath the windowsill. On the other wall there is a desk with shelves above it; between the desk and the bed there is barely enough space to walk. If we had ever thought to reallocate rooms according to size rather than seniority, I would have spent my time in here. Julian grew, eventually, to five foot eleven and a half; I am five foot two.

My brother first outgrew me when I was fourteen and he was twelve, which means we would have had to swap rooms in 1984. That would have been fair until 1991, when I finished my degree, moved back home and began to commute to my first job. I hadn't meant to come back – it felt humiliating – but as I spent my twenties moving in and out of postgraduate courses and poorly paid jobs, scuttling off brightly to yet another town only to come trudging home again, I kept finding myself waking up in my old room, the room at the back on the right-hand side. I loathed it more and more, but I needed it. I still needed it.

Julian, on the other hand, did more than outgrow me; he outran me too. He spent the whole middle year of his degree in the States, travelling when he wasn't studying. At the end of his third year he won a scholarship to Yale, and moved into the first of several student houses in New Haven, Connecticut. He turned left, he went West, and he never lived on either side of the landing again.

In 2008, the room is a forlorn hybrid, half eighteen-year-old boy's bedroom and half junk room. My mother has had extra shelves put up on the left-hand wall, to store some of the books overflowing from the rest of the house, and the bed is covered with her half-finished needlework projects. But the posters I bought back for him from the Soviet Union have remained on the walls, the tatty Emu puppet and beaten-up Snoopy doll are still lolling on top of the wardrobe, and the shelves above his desk still hold the books that never made it to America.

I need to fill a box. Giselle should have a box, to help her piece together who her father was. I put my hand up on top of the wardrobe, meaning to take Snoopy, but I touch something else instead, something rougher, and when I pull it down I see that it's Julian's blue-and-white rabbit, which our aunt and uncle gave him when he was born – the first thing he ever owned. So I take that. I also take down the green plush hippo pyjama case, only because I always liked it.

Then I sit down on the bed and take a look at the desk unit. All the books here were Julian's. There are the interactive adventure books he used to devour as schoolboy, the 1980s equivalent of long-form video games. There's a little collection of novels by Stanislaw Lem – my brother, like my parents, loved science fiction – I was the odd one out in that respect. There is a *Tanakh* – a copy of the Bible in Hebrew, a bar mitzvah present he never used. Next to the *Tanakh* are two large, hardback *Peanuts* collections, which I decide to take home for my son.

∗
∗

Anything to do with *Peanuts* was serious currency in our extended family: children could be bribed, rewarded or consoled with Snoopy dolls; birthdays meant cards with Charlie Brown or Pig-Pen or Sally or Woodstock on the front. My first watch had asymmetrical Snoopy arms instead of hands. On Saturdays, when in theory we should have been in synagogue reading the *Tanakh*, we were in Brent Cross Shopping Centre buying anything to do with *Peanuts*. I was the serious paperback collector (I have already boxed up the eighty-odd I've been keeping in my old room) but Julian had a few of his own. As well as the big treasuries, I find a big, square 'family celebration book' called *Brothers & Sisters: It's All Relative*. Its stars were Charlie Brown and his sister Sally, Snoopy and his sister Belle and brother Spike, and of course Lucy and Linus. Linus was the little brother with the blue security blanket, and Lucy was the bossy big sister who was always trying to take it away.

⁎⁎

The first time I saw the *Brothers & Sisters* book it was sitting on a dull green hospital bedspread in the men's surgical ward at Edgware General, where my brother was recovering from an emergency appendectomy. He was seventeen, in the sixth form. I was home from university and had taken two buses so that I could see him by myself, without Mum.

'It must be weird, being here as patient,' I said. 'Do you remember Mum taking us, when she used to work here?'

'Yeah, the office was at the top of a ramp – didn't we used to race cars down it?'

'And there was that room halfway down the ramp – the Appliance Officer—'

'Only we thought it was "Appliance officer"…'

'… who was in charge of the apples!'

My brother laughed and then grimaced. His wound was stapled, and whenever he laughed, it hurt. I said how daft it was of Auntie Marian to have given him the *Peanuts* book, under the circumstances, and that made him laugh again – which made me laugh because I knew I shouldn't – we couldn't look at each other, which reminded us of all the other times we hadn't been able to look at each other, which made us laugh again – which was difficult for him because it hurt, and difficult for me, because I didn't want to hurt him. I remember how his face was contorted that day – half laughter, half pain.

*
**

If it were up to me, if there were no practical considerations, I think I would take every little thing my brother owned. Each in its own way partakes of the lived experience of some earlier version of him: the tiny child who cuddled a blue-and-white rabbit; the ten-year-old who went on interactive adventures and read *Peanuts*; the bar mitzvah boy who read an extra Torah portion so that a Jewish boy in the USSR could participate by proxy. In the drawers of the desk unit I find the dissection tools he used for his biology A level, and I take those for Giselle. I find the child's *tallis* (prayer shawl) he wore before his bar mitzvah and I take that too.

There's one more drawer. I pull it open and find it stuffed with old cassette tapes. At first I assume they must be music recordings, taped copies Julian made so that he could listen to his LPs on his Walkman, but when I take one out I realize that these are examples of another kind of obsolete technology. When my brother was twelve or so, he graduated from interactive reading to computer gaming. He had an Atari and then a Commodore (or perhaps it was a Commodore and then an Atari?). On Saturdays, instead of going to Brent Cross and buying *Peanuts* merchandise, he would get Dad to drive him to Radio Shack in Golders Green, where he would buy computer games on cassette tape.

Gaming was a time-consuming hobby then. It required commitment and technical know-how. You had to load the games onto the computer every time you wanted to play them; this would take several minutes at least, and all the time the cassette drive would emit a tortured screeching noise, as if it were complaining about the effort. What you got at the end of this process were simple, low-resolution games like *Space Invaders* and *Dancing Demon*. There was one called *Robot Wars* which took particularly long to load because – and Julian told me this in hushed tones – it was written in something he called machine code, understood only by computers themselves and very few humans. I remember thinking at the time that it was hardly worth the trouble: the robots didn't even move, just stood on either side of the screen firing little hyphens out of guns they held in their unmoving robot hands.

I don't know who, in 2008, would want these games. I don't know what on earth they would use to play them. They belong in a museum, but I can't think of a museum that would take them. Someone somewhere probably collects these things, but I wouldn't know how to reach them. I have no excuse to hang on to them, no good reason not to throw them away – but they hold traces of my brother in their obsolete code, and even though I haven't thought of them for years, it hurts to have to abandon them now.

*
**

I also have to abandon the remains of another old technology. There's a crate of vinyl LPs under the shelf and I don't have any room for it at home. This troubles me less than the drawerful of old computer games, partly because any records from my brother's collection that I liked migrated into mine years ago, with his blessing. He usually discovered bands first, and then introduced me to them. The cassette tape of Tears for Fears' *The Hurting*, which we used to pester our parents into playing in the car on the way to our grandparents', was his before it was mine.

That album, and the title track especially, are plaited tightly with memories of Julian. After he moved to the States, we managed to keep having the conversations we could only have with each other, but instead of sitting on his bed or mine, we used the phone. Once I picked up the receiver, heard nothing but the first notes of the *Bagpuss* theme tune, and realized that no one but my brother could be calling.

Another time, I answered to the beginning of the title track from *The Hurting*. When we got to the chorus we both joined in and sang in concert, from either side of the Atlantic:

the hu-ur-ur-ur

ur-ur ur-ur

the hu-ur-ur-ur

ur-ur ur-ur…

I don't think that song was ever meant to be funny. And when Julian died, I kept remembering two lines from that same song, one of many lyrics that acquired a new and unbearable meaning, and it wasn't funny at all:

Is it an horrific dream?

Am I sinking fast?

.*.

Why did my brother sink so very fast, so completely? The question worries at us. I keep asking my therapist what she thinks; my mother keeps asking me.

Do you think he had a gambling problem? Compulsive gambling was something of a family trait, handed down the male line. Our Great-grandfather Limburg was a bookmaker who bet his own profits away. His middle son, our grandfather, bet his workplace's Christmas-club money on a losing horse and had to pawn my grandmother's engagement ring. On weekends, I remember how he and Dad would do the pools with the same ferocious intensity. It was difficult to get my dad away from slot machines on holiday.

It was difficult to pull Julian away too. I tell Mum I have absolutely no idea if it was gambling, and no way of knowing either.

Do you think he was confused about his sexuality? In the eighties, the *Sun* and *News of the World* started giving away bingo cards with every issue, so my dad kept buying them. My mother protested every time, but it wasn't until the *News of the World* printed an artist's impression of what they called the 'Vicarage Rape' that she finally prevailed. Hundreds of photos of topless women must have passed through the house by then. One day, when I was talking to my brother in his room, I opened up our old marble tin and found one hidden in there. Julian turned crimson, his hands flew to his cheeks, and he begged me not to tell Mum.

I never did, and I don't tell her now, though I do say that I'm reasonably sure he wasn't in the closet. And I take the marble tin, which these days holds nothing but marbles, home with me for my son.

⁎⁎

At the back of my mother's overladen wardrobe shelf, hidden behind the floppy-brimmed red hat that she used to wear to synagogue, we find an old Safeway carrier bag, stuffed full of photographs. After supper, with my mother's permission, I upend the bag onto the living-room carpet, which instantly swarms with old versions of the four of us. Most are pictures of me, Julian or the two of us together. The oldest pictures are of a tiny, wrinkly baby in a fluffy white Babygro which is far too big for it. There are seven of these altogether, each showing the baby striking a minutely different pose, but my father has written the same words on all seven backs: *Joanne, four weeks.* These are first baby photos, taken by excited first-time parents: we have a set of photos of our son which, colour aside, look strikingly similar. Julian, the second child, doesn't appear until he is already some way into babyhood, sitting up, adorably plump in a way that I never managed, and usually placed next to me.

He always knew he was the least important... These words keep barging into my head. I feel the need to disprove them, so I'm reassured – a little – to find that, once we are past toddlerhood, there must be as many solo images of my brother as there are of me.

'Look,' I say to Ayako in my head, 'he was *terribly* important: my grandmother's holding him in this one, and you can see she loves him; this is him in a new jacket; in the paddling pool; on the beach with a spade; on a Spacehopper; all by himself in a pedalo; looking out of my bedroom window; holding up a cake he's made by himself. Here he is fishing; here he is in the south of France with spindly thirteen-year-old legs; with his friends on a school trip. And in most of these – do you see? – he's *smiling...*'

Mum says I can take the photos home with me; she has gone without looking at them for so many years and she can do without looking at them now. When we find my brother's GCSE certificates among the photos, she shocks me by suggesting that we might as well throw them away. I know it makes no practical sense to keep them, but I don't want them to go the way of the cassette-tape computer games. My brother worked for those certificates; his cohort was the first to do the new GCSEs and I remember how scary it was for him, with his future depending on an experiment. I add them to Giselle's box.

⁂

Between us, Julian's widow and I hold the two parts of his life history, in our memories and our photograph albums. I want my niece to have the full story, a father she can remember entire, and I mean to make sure that she has him. Back in Cambridge, I empty the carrier bag full of pictures that I took from the family home, pick out all the photographs I can find with my brother in them and arrange them, as best I can, in date order. Then I take my own albums down from the shelf, extract more photographs of Julian and use them to fill in the gaps in the timeline. Now I have a picture narrative that takes him from babyhood to his PhD award. I add a photograph of the family home and download photographs of Julian's primary and secondary schools so that Giselle can see them too. I rip the relevant page out of an old A–Z and draw an arrow on it to the cul-de-sac where we grew up together.

Then I go out to the shops. An assistant in the art-supplies shop finds me a hardbound sketchbook with acid-free paper, the right kind of glue and a pen with ink that won't fade. I take my collection of pictures to a photographic shop where I'm told that to produce high-quality copies of such old photographs without access to negatives will be time-consuming and expensive. I don't mind that at all: I want it to cost me.

When I have the photographs back, with their expensive replicas, I take the scrapbook, glue and pen out of the bag and start work. I get as far as pasting in and annotating the *A–Z* extract and the pictures of the house and schools before I have to stop. The distance between the brother in the photographs and the dead brother is at once too great and not nearly great enough. I put all the carefully gathered tools and images away. Five years will pass before I can bear to take them out again.

Vessel Eight

Q: What is *yahrzeit?*

A: *We observe* yahrzeit *on the anniversary of the death of a parent, spouse, sibling or child, in accordance with the Jewish calendar. On that day, the family recite Kaddish for the deceased family member, and light a* yahrzeit *candle, which burns for twenty-four hours inside a glass. Lost loved ones can also be remembered communally, at* yizkor, *or memorial services which are held on Yom Kippur, Passover, Shavuoth* and the eighth day of Sukkoth, and* yyahrzeit *candles are lit shortly before Yom Kippur eve. If the deceased is buried within easy travelling distance, the family can visit the grave and pray there.*

*
**

My mother would visit her parents at the Orthodox cemetery in Edmonton, and our father at the Reform Synagogues' cemetery in Cheshunt. I haven't been back there since her stone was consecrated on its plot next to his. I would, if it were within easy travelling distance, or I believed that any part of them were really there.

When our grandfather was hit by the bus and killed in 1941, our grandmother was discouraged from buying the next plot.

---

* Shavuoth commemorates the revelation of the Torah on Mount Sinai.

Although we are expected to remember our dead, and pray for them, we are also supposed to accept that they are gone and get on with life without them. Our grandmother never could; she bought that plot, never married again and sought the services of a medium, so that she might keep a tighter grip on the memory of her husband.

∗∗

Julian died on the 13th of Av 5768. In 2009, his *yahrzeit* falls on 3 August, and in 2010 on 24 July. I keep a stock of memorial candles in the house but can never make a positive decision to light them. That would mean acceptance, and I'm not anywhere near ready for that.

∗∗

Bang! The door of the classroom slammed open and there was my little brother, in his puffy green anorak with the hood up, grinning all over his chubby face. Everyone laughed. He was obviously thrilled to see me, to be giving me this big surprise at school. I didn't know where to look.

Mum appeared just behind him and shepherded him in.

'Sorry,' she said to Mrs Baker. 'He's very excited to see Joanne at school!'

Now everyone knew who he was. They all turned round to stare at me, and laughed harder. Look at Joanne: she picks her face! she chews her hair! she always knocks her milk over! she uses long words! she gets told off for daydreaming! she plays with boys! and now she's got a brother! and he's weird too!

Mrs Baker smiled at my brother.

'You must be Julian.'

He was shy now. His fingers were in his mouth, and he just nodded.

'So are you coming to reception next term?'

Another nod.

'That's lovely! I think you'll do really well – especially if you're as clever as your sister.'

So of course they all turned round and smirked at me again.

⁘

Not long back from Plainsville, I am trying to re-establish my old routines. This includes parenting duties, and these are not straightforward. Getting our five-year-old son to bed, for example, is a major undertaking. He resists and delays for as long as he can: he wants crackers, he wants milk, he needs to go to the toilet, he has – oh Lord – a question, for which he requires an immediate and full answer, preferably one that will lead to another question. He expects both parents to be present while he hears his bedtime story – or two, or three – and then whichever parent has read will stay on for a time, that time being as long as he can make it. 'Who's doing the reading and staying tonight?' he asks.

Tonight I've read the story, so I'm the one who stays. Usually he likes to sit next to me or on top of me and talk about things, but he's in a more boisterous mood this evening, and is throwing himself about on the bed to show me how he can fall over on purpose and not hurt himself. He shows me a forward roll. He tries to show me a backwards roll and ends up kicking me in the face, hard, with both feet. It hurts. I yelp. My new, expensive glasses slide off my face and hit the floor. When I pick them up, one of the arms is sticking out at a strange angle. They'll need fixing.

'Sorry, Mummy – it was an accident.' He looks as he always does when he thinks I'm hurt: concerned and a little afraid. I start to do what I always do, which is to reassure him.

'It's all right, darling. I'm…' No, I'm not fine. My nose throbs and now my eyes are leaking. My son is staring at me. He can't decide what to do with his face. Eventually his voice comes out, very wobbly, very small.

'Why are you crying? Grown-ups don't cry.'

'I'm sorry. Sometimes we do. I… it's nothing you've done, it's not your fault – I'm just very sad about my brother, and when you're very sad, sometimes even tiny things like glasses needing mending can make you cry, even grown-ups.'

'I understand,' he says, not because he does, but because he doesn't want me to say any more. We are both of us at a loss. I call his father up, to do some staying without tears, and fix this broken bedtime.

*
*

Nikki phones.

'Look, I know you don't want to go to your mum's flat, and I do understand why – I know it's really hard for you – but she really wants you to see it. Every time she comes round she's going on about "Joanne hasn't come to see the flat yet. I'd really like Joanne to come and see the flat. I don't know why Joanne hasn't come to the flat yet – she said she was busy but now she's finished the book. I'm so pleased with the flat but I do wish Joanne—"'

'I get it. I'm sorry. I'll go and see the flat.'

Mum's new home is on the ground floor of one of the many blocks on Ballards Lane, a short walk from West Finchley Tube station ('So you can get there easily from King's Cross.'). She has a parking space and her own front door, but there are no stairs to climb and no need to garden. She's much closer to her friends now. She's freed up some much-needed capital. This flat is perfect for her. I wish she'd never moved.

I don't say that. When she shows me the small, spare room, I don't say that the books from the old house which line its walls put me in mind of the disoriented elderly relatives I've visited in nursing homes. Instead I say what a good size it is. I admire the large, square living room and the master bedroom with its built-in wardrobes – *so* much storage! I agree that the bathroom could do with some work. I approve all the changes she's made in the kitchen. I pretend not to have noticed all the pictures of Giselle she has pinned up on the corkboard with the bills and the shopping lists.

Later that night, after we've eaten all the food we've bought from Waitrose (she's only a short walk from Waitrose!) and watched *High Society* on DVD, we make up a folding bed for me in the living room and say good night.

As my mother knows, I have finished my book, but I have already started work on another. I have decided – much to my own surprise – to write a book about Queen Anne. It doesn't occur to me that this might be because I need desperately to get away from my own story for a while. At this point, I am not sure whether it is going to be non-fiction or fiction, but in either case it is obvious that I know next to nothing about the period and am going to have to research everything from scratch. At the moment I'm in the middle of reading a book about London life in 1700.[*] When I get into bed and take the bookmark out, I see that I'm at the beginning of a new chapter: 'Death'.

Most of the chapter is concerned with funerals, which were important social events. The body would be viewed at the family home before being carried in procession through the streets to the churchyard, where the mourners would stay to watch the interment. The custom was to bury the body face up in a grave that was oriented east to west, so that the dead relative was prepared for his eventual resurrection on Judgement Day – except for suicides.

If the corpse of a suicide was accepted into the churchyard at all, it was buried face down in a north–south grave on the north side of the yard. More often, they were buried naked at crossroads with stakes thrust through them. Suicides were committed at the

---

[*]   Maureen Waller, *1700: Scenes from London Life* (London: Sceptre, 2001).

devil's prompting; the spirit of a person who died in this way was bound to be a restless, malevolent entity that would menace the living. It was important to carry out the burial in such a way as to prevent this mischief, and to make sure that the suicide would be unable to rise on Judgement Day. The burial of a suicide was a gory public spectacle, like a hanging…

I close the book. Suddenly I want very much to speak to my mother about Julian; more than that – I need to. I can hear her moving about the flat, so I get up and go to find her. She's in the kitchen, pulling the blind down for the night.

'Hello,' she says. 'Are you OK? I thought you'd gone to bed.'

'I had,' I said. 'But you know…'

'Mm-hmm?'

'Is that the new kitchen blind up already?'

'Yes. What do you think?'

'I really like it. It's nice. A good choice. Can I just get a glass of water?'

∗∗

My thirty-ninth birthday is coming up, on 3 April. As usual, Mum starts asking me what I want in February. As usual, I have no idea.

'Posh bath stuff?' I say finally, towards the end of March. 'I always like that.'

'A trip to Crabtree & Evelyn?'

'Yes. That'll be nice. Thank you.'

So Mum takes me to the posh smell shop.

'Get whatever you like!' Mum says. 'Don't worry about the price!'

She would love me to be greedy, I can see that. She would love me to want the expensive bath gel very, very much, so that I can be delighted when she buys it for me. At moments like this, I am aware of the power I have as the one remaining child, and I feel as if it shames both of us.

I pick a few things out. I look pleased with my haul and tell Mum how much I'll enjoy using them. It's lovely to have a mother who is able and willing to buy me expensive things. I have a bag full of them now. It's my fault entirely if I still feel empty.

**

My little boy is on my lap in the living room, crying loudly and inconsolably. Our long-haired white cat has recovered well from her leg surgery, and has demonstrated this by seizing a blackbird chick out of the air as it falls from the nest. My son has witnessed this at very close quarters, chased the cat into the house, screaming, 'Get it off her!' and then watched me fail to rescue the chick, whose corpse the cat has just dropped on the floor. It is altogether the most shocking thing he has ever seen.

'Is it dead, Mummy?'

'I'm afraid it is, yes.'

He cries all the harder. 'I don't want her in this house! I only want the other cat! She's a bird-killer!'

I explain that the bird was a baby that fell out of a nest, that baby birds who fall out of nests never survive, that the bigger birds he saw were trying to fight the cat off but couldn't, that birds were part of nature and so were cats, and in nature bigger animals like cats often ate smaller animals like birds, that the cat was only doing what was in her nature to do, that she wasn't evil on purpose. I tell him that the parent birds have lots of other babies, they have lots of babies every year, and that even though some eggs get broken and some chicks fall out of the nest, they still have other children and they will be all right.

'But they must be sad,' he says. 'I have to go out and cheer them up.'

We go back into the garden. My son walks to the back, where the branches of the horse chestnut tree where the late chick lived spread over our fence, and holds up both his hands, like an orator addressing his people.

'Little bird,' he begins, 'I'm so sorry that you lost your baby, but please don't be sad, you still have your other children.' He looks back at me. 'Do you think they might be crying now?'

'They might.'

'Shall we bury their baby for them?'

'OK.'

I fetch the corpse of the baby bird and bury it in a flowerbed. My son names it 'Fall-y', and says goodbye to it. I find a brick to serve as a gravestone, and write the name on it. My son draws a picture and writes, 'Died 1', because Fall-y was one when he died.

He finds an empty bubble-mixture bottle with bird crap on it and offers it to the parents as a reminder of 'Fall-y, who died'. Then he shouts at the cat in human and bird language.

'I'M A GIANT BIRD!' he yells. The cat runs away, to his obvious satisfaction. Now she knows how it feels.

⁑

Early in 2010, my mother tells me she has 'hit a wall'. She has been coping as well as she can, but now she seems to be more and more tearful, is having trouble sleeping. She would rather be up and out and doing, but the enormity of her grief has finally reduced her to down and in and feeling. A doctor at the Older People's Mental Health Service – she says the words 'Older People's' with rueful irony – has prescribed Mirtazapine, a strong antidepressant, and for the first time since her childhood sessions at the Tavistock, she has agreed that it might be helpful to 'talk to someone'. The nature of Julian's death, the tension between the two of them in the months leading up to it, the lack of contact with her grandchild in the months that have followed, her back pain, her osteoporosis, the unavoidable time spent in her flat alone with the thoughts she doesn't want to have, which threaten to overwhelm her…

'I think it should be helpful,' she says.

'Yes,' I say. 'I think it should.'

'And for the guilt, for coming to terms with the lack of answers…'

'I've found therapy helpful for that. It doesn't make it go away but—'

'… it helps you to work through it.'

My mother has a new set of objectives – that helps her too.

※

It doesn't make it go away… especially not when your memory is still compiling its case against you. From the files:

If I had only hit my brother and cut up his blanket, that would have been bad enough. But I did worse.

When I was nine, I started writing poems and stories in exercise books that I bought from the newsagent's. I was proud of my efforts and my parents encouraged me. Understandably, Julian wanted to try as well. I can still remember the sentence my seven-year-old brother wrote in *his* exercise book and read out to me and our mother:

Billy stood at the side of the canal, looking at the long boats and narrow boats.

I laughed and said it was RUBBISH! Julian burst into tears. After he died, of all the things I ever did to him as a mean older sister, it was this that seemed like the worst. Why couldn't I let him write a sentence in a notebook and be pleased about it? Would it have *killed* me to allow him a voice?

※

In the summer of 1990, when I was two years into my degree,

my brother took his A levels. The day the results arrived he had a terrible shock: according to the slip that came through the door, he had received an A, a B and a D, which meant that he wouldn't be able to go to his first choice, a course at East Anglia which included a middle year in America, the course he had set his heart on.

I remember him sitting on the floor with his back to the sofa, his head in his hands, while I tried to console him by talking up his second choice. I was appalled to see him like that, but at the same time, at the back of my mind, there lurked the thought that, although it was a shock for him, the prospect of failing to achieve an ambition couldn't annihilate my brother like it would surely have annihilated me. And as the D turned out to be a printing error, it would be a long time before I would realize how wrong I'd been; how stupidly, complacently wrong.

*
*

In late spring, Mum tells me that the Community Mental Health Team have now discharged her.

'Already? You didn't want any more sessions?'

'No, I'm doing so much better now – I'm sleeping more and crying less. The way I put it to the psychologist was that I'm feeling more proportionate about the conflict between me and your brother before he died – do you know what I mean?'

'Proportionate. Yes.'

'I said I don't find myself spiralling down through the negative thoughts so much. Of course I'm still feeling low about it all, but...'

'Of course you are. I'm glad the treatment helped. Would you say you were feeling more yourself·now?'

'Yes. Definitely. But tell me about you. How are you?'

'The same – still feeling low about it.'

'Well, of course you are.'

∗∗

My brother and I were standing in front of the fridge-freezer, arguing about something I can't remember. He was in his late teens and I in my early twenties. He shouted:

'… and that's just typical of you, making a mess of your life!'

Mum was there too. She called a halt to the row and made my brother apologize, but I could never un-hear Julian's words, nor could I ever forget how I must have appeared to him, when I was in my early twenties. You're not supposed to have to worry about an older sibling. And he did worry about me, his whole life.

Leave Joanne alone! She's fragile!

∗∗

… but all the time he was the most fragile of all of us.

Sometime in 2007, when I was most deeply absorbed in my work on *The Woman Who Thought Too Much*, Julian phoned to tell me that he had been diagnosed with Adult Attention Deficit Disorder. I was bewildered.

'But how come you've done so well?'

'It's not about that. It's nothing to do with not applying yourself. What I do is I "hyperfocus", which means I can really concentrate on certain things, like my research, but now that I've got to parallel process so much, with teaching, and managing the lab – well, I'm struggling. I feel overwhelmed. I'll be in a meeting and I'll just drift off...'

'I'm sorry... is there treatment?'

'They've prescribed me this drug to take a couple of times a day – it's like, a really low dose of amphetamine.'

'What, like *speed*? You know Dad failed his accountancy exams when he took that.'

'It's a low, controlled dose – it helps concentration.'

'Oh, OK.'

'And about Dad. I think he had it too. I think the whole family do. You, Mum – all of us. It explains a lot, doesn't it?'

'All of us? That changes my story then, doesn't it? I'll have to do some more research... Can I put your diagnosis in the book?'

'No, *please* don't! They don't know at work!'

He sounded terrified. I said I would say that an unnamed relative had been diagnosed, and he agreed to that. I'm still ashamed of my self-centred writer's response to his news. When he told Mum about his diagnosis, she had even more trouble believing it, and was horrified by the prescription he'd been given. He didn't take it for long, though – he realized it was making him paranoid.

And by the time I finished the book, he was no longer alive to care about what I'd written.

*
**

Shortly before the memoir comes out in spring 2010, I attend a conference run by OCD Action for sufferers and their families. I am one of the few people to attend alone, and I remain on my own. There are couples there, daughters with their mothers, delegations from local support groups. In most cases, it's not obvious who suffers and who doesn't, though I do see some people who look haunted, who walk painfully slowly with their hands turned inwards, so as not to touch anything. At lunchtime I have a brief chat with a woman who spends at least an hour checking locks and switches every night before she can allow herself to go to bed. She asks me what form my OCD takes, and when I explain how I fear for my safety and my son's, she comments that my anxieties sound pretty normal to her. I don't know quite how to continue the conversation after that, so I'm relieved that lunch has come to an end and it's time to join our afternoon workshop groups. I attend one on how to set up and run support groups. The question arises: what if someone in the group is clearly suicidal? The answer is that you have to get them straight to A & E. You need professionals to cope with suicide.

I go home wondering if my book will help anyone I saw at the conference, and feeling – after my conversation with the checking woman – a little fraudulent. That night I have another of my recurrent dreams, the one in which I'm living with my mother and studying for my A levels again. As usual, I haven't managed to get to a single lesson all year and, also as usual, I have slowly come to remember that I already have A levels, and resolve to send a message to the school to tell them I won't be coming back.

At this point the dream takes an unusual turn. A car draws up outside my childhood home with the psychiatrist in it – apparently one of us has called him for help with my depression. I get into the passenger seat and start talking about how I don't want to go back to school, why I think this is the right decision. As I talk, I get a sudden vision of myself shaving in the shower, and at the very same time I find myself thinking of my brother. I tell the psychiatrist about the vision and say that I thought I looked marmoreal in that moment, like a fresh corpse.

In an instant, I hear the psychiatrist activate the car's central locks – thud! 'That's my evening gone,' he says. 'I was going out to dinner, but now I have to drive you straight to a psychiatric hospital.' He phones my mother to tell her that I am in a suicidal crisis, it is an emergency, and then he drives me away.

⁂

By summer 2010, the seam of poetry about brother-loss that I have been so diligently mining is beginning to run out. It occurs to me that perhaps I don't want to write about Julian any more, at least not for the time being, but this thought strikes me as heretical. Besides, I don't really feel moved to write about anything else; at this stage, Queen Anne is still just a research project. When my brother is not occupying my mind, it feels dangerously empty. I have hollowed myself out to give him room in the living world.

And he has superimposed himself on my son. Several times a day, I refer to him as 'Julian'. I think of his bedroom, at the front of the house, as 'Julian's room'. There is a slight resemblance between them facially – my son has the distinctive Eurasian eye shape that my brother and I shared. He also has the daft excitability that my brother had as child, but these little similarities can't adequately account for the slips I'm making.

It infuriates Chris when I use the wrong name. I explain that I can't help it, and add that my father used to make the same mistake. I joke that, for a long time, I thought my name was "Marian – er, Ruth? – no, Joanne!", but Chris doesn't find it funny. And when the owner of the wrong name is prematurely dead, I suppose it isn't.

'You do have a problem with the masculine in your family,' my therapist says, reminding me of various stories I have told her: about my widowed grandmother's attempts to undermine my uncle's relationship with my aunt, about the emotional demands my mother made on my brother after our father died.

'Well, men have been at a premium,' I say. 'They don't seem to last very long: my grandfather died young, then my dad dropped dead, and now Julian... My father died in the middle of the night, and when I first moved in with Chris, I used to listen to him breathing – I was scared that it could stop any time... When Julian was finding Mum difficult, he used to say, "I'm not Dad! I can't be Dad!" She used to phone him if she couldn't sleep – he would come home tired from work, and then Mum would call him up and dump on him. But she dumped on me as well, you know!'

'I know she did. But I want to stay on the subject of the men in your family.'

'They're very precious.'

'Yes, they are.'

'And vulnerable.'

'That too.'

'I'm scared for my son.'

'I know.'

'But he's not my brother.'

'No. He isn't. And he can't be.'

∴

The Lord hath trodden under foot all my mighty men in the midst of me: he hath called an assembly against me to crush my young men… (Lamentations, 1: 15)

∴

Summer 2010. My mother has been having problems with her heart: atrial fibrillation and palpitations. Her GP sends her to a cardiologist, who runs some tests and discovers that her blood-calcium levels are very much higher than they should be. It is most likely the result of benign tumours on her parathyroid glands, the tiny organs in the neck that would normally regulate levels of calcium. She may need surgery, but the priority for the time being is to reduce the levels of blood-calcium, so she is admitted to Barnet General Hospital for twenty-four hours, where she can be attached to the bisphosphonate drip that will treat the hypercalcaemia.

She doesn't need me to come down, she says. And yes, it's fine for us to go away on holiday.

So, a few days later, we are on the beach at North Berwick. Chris and the boy are rock-pooling. I am sitting by myself with a takeaway coffee in my hand, watching eider ducks ride the waves and listening out for the peeeeep of an oystercatcher. We have been out to the Bass Rock on a boat and seen the gannets wheeling about above us, folding themselves into sharp white missiles and diving for fish. A little squadron of puffins escorted the boat for a couple of hundred yards on the return journey, a wish perfectly granted.

My phone buzzes in my handbag. It's my cousin.

'Hi, Joanne, it's Nikki. I don't want you to worry or anything, and Mum said I shouldn't tell you, but I did think you should know that she's in hospital.'

'In hospital? Why? Is it the parathyroid thing again?'

'No. Pneumonia.'

'What?'

'Oh, don't worry – she's fine, she's going to be fine. I just thought you'd want to know.'

*
**

I phone my mother. She answers straight away and sounds like herself. It was naughty of my cousin to have called me, no we shouldn't interrupt the holiday, yes she is fine, she'll be out soon, it's all just a pain really.

'You want to know the weirdest thing?' she asks. 'I've had a chest X-ray, there were some shadows – no, don't worry! – and they turned out to be tuberculosis scars!'

'I didn't know you had TB.'

'Well I didn't know I'd had it either, it was quite a shock.'

'I can imagine. But how can someone have TB and not even know?'

'I was young and healthy – it was when I was working at St Mary's on the TB ward. I must have caught it from a patient, thought it was a bout of flu or something and just shrugged it off.'

'Well, I never… Could it come back?'

'No… It might have weakened my lungs a bit, who knows, but it's not worth worrying about. I'm fine, my temperature's come right down already.'

She says again that she'll be home soon. I promise that when I get back from Scotland I'll travel on to London alone so we can spend a few days together.

'Something to look forward to,' she says. 'Honestly, with this and the parathyroid and my heart valve – I feel like I'm falling apart!'

*
**

But when I arrive at the flat, Mum is feeling unwell again.

'They said to phone them,' she tells me, 'but I'm not sure if I want to. If I phone them, they'll tell me to go in, and if I go in, they might admit me.'

'But you know you should phone,' I say.

We are sitting next to each other on the sofa, staring at the receiver on the coffee table, as if it could provide us with the answer to our dilemma.

'I know!' She's close to tears. 'But I don't want to go to hospital! I was looking forward to this weekend with you.'

'You should phone. You never know, they might not take you in this time – they might give you some pills or whatever and send you home.'

She does phone, and they do call her in. Instead of going out to eat, as planned, we take a cab straight to the A & E department in Barnet General. They are expecting my mother, so as soon as we arrive we are shown through into a long corridor with curtained beds along one side. Mum gets onto one of the beds, the curtains are drawn all the way round, and her processing as hospital meat begins, with clipboards and blood pressure monitors and the first of many stethoscopes. She is telling everyone who comes in that she is not going to be staying here tonight, but we both know that it is no longer up to her – they have taken her details and tagged her wrist; she is theirs to dispose of.

After a little while, a junior doctor comes in to tell us that Mum is to be sent upstairs to the Clinical Decisions Unit. Mum rolls her eyes and groans, 'Great! In that case, if previous form is anything to go by, I'll be here all night.'

In the meantime, she needs to vacate the triage space she is occupying, so she is wheeled to the X-ray waiting area down the corridor. As we arrive, another bed with an elderly woman on it is trundled out of the X-ray suite and left in the bay with us. The woman is fast asleep, with her teeth out, snoring loudly. I wonder if she was even aware that she was being X-rayed. I imagine that she would be mortified if she knew that she had been abandoned in a public place, snoring, without her teeth.

The poor snoring woman exhibit serves as a preview for the Clinical Decisions Unit, which is a pitiful geriatric zoo. Everywhere you look, there's a patient lying splay-legged on the beds, like a discarded rag doll. A man in a wheelchair is insisting, again and again, that he hasn't had his tea yet and asking where is it, don't they know, he was supposed to have had it, what's happened to his tea? The woman opposite us in our four-bed bay is shouting 'Nurse! Nurse! Nurse!' without stopping. From time to time a nurse will approach her, to reassure her that she hasn't been forgotten and ask her please to stop shouting – there's no need, is there? After these interventions, we get a brief, peaceful pause, then the inevitable resumption of 'Nurse! Nurse! Nurse!'

In sharp contrast is a woman of about my age, occupying the opposite corner of the bay, fully clothed and in command of every faculty, making energetic phone calls to all her family members; just because she's been admitted to hospital, it doesn't mean that she should give up micromanaging. She is holding fast to her family and her role within it; she is holding on to herself. It takes strength of character to do that once you've been fed into the hospital machinery. My mother is also hanging on to herself, just, by reading books on her Kindle and giving me her opinion of the running of the ward. As a medical social worker, she has been a hospital insider for decades. She can identify herself with the staff rather than the helpless patients.

But only up to a point. As far as the staff are concerned, her blood-test results count for more than her opinions, and what they say is that she needs another bisphosphonate infusion. She will have to stay in. When a doctor finally sits down next to the bed and tells her this, Mum dissolves into tears.

'What if I decide to go home?' she says, 'I don't want to stay in hospital. Can't I come back tomorrow and have the treatment as an outpatient?'

The doctor, a very young woman surely not long qualified, looks taken aback.

'Well, in theory, yes, but we wouldn't advise it – we need to observe you, and tomorrow is a Saturday...'

'But I don't want to stay in hospital!'

Mum puts her head in her hands. I put an arm round her shoulders. Over the top of her head, I meet the doctor's eyes, asking me to please help.

'Mum,' I say, 'I know you don't want to stay in, I know it's horrible, but it does sound like the sensible thing to do and it won't be for long… I'll come back tomorrow and stay for all the visiting hours… You know it's the right thing to do.'

Mum agrees, then apologizes to the doctor for making a fuss and asks a nurse to please call her daughter a taxi. It's three in the morning. For the first but not the last time, I enter the flat alone.

⁂

When I go to visit Mum the next day, with my uncle and aunt, she is back to being the mother I recognize. She has managed to get a room by herself. As we enter, she is talking to one of her friends on her mobile. There is a thoroughly read copy of the *Guardian* on her bed.

I hand her the toiletries, clothes and books she has asked for, from the flat. My uncle and aunt sit down on the two plastic chairs that, with the bed, stand and the drip attached to my mother, make up the entirety of the furniture in the room. I perch on the edge of the bed.

My uncle points to the *Guardian*. 'So, what's getting your goat at the moment, Ruth?'

We are a few months into the Coalition government and its austerity policies, so my mother has more than enough to say.

'What would have happened to the two of us under a government like this? If we'd had student loans and tuition fees – we'd never have got to university in the first place!'

My uncle turns to me. 'I had to persuade your grandmother

to let your mother go to university. She thought it was a waste of time for girls.'

'Mum's told me that. She wanted you to take a secretarial course?'

'Most of the other girls in my grammar-school class did. They got married at nineteen, twenty, twenty-one, never really worked. I escaped that fate, thank God.'

'And why do you think you managed to make that escape, Ruth?'

'Because I was bright,' my mother says, with great emphasis.

I offer to go for coffee. By the time I get back, with my cappuccino and Mum's latte, the talk has turned to mutual acquaintances I've never heard of, and plans for holidays.

∗∗

It was ever thus. I remember my brother sighing at the prospect of a day with relatives:

'Oh great, another afternoon of listening to them talk about Jewish people we don't know.'

If he were here in the hospital, we would roll our eyes at each other, and try not to giggle.

∗∗

Autumn 2010 begins very badly, with a loud thud and the yowl of a frightened animal. I run down from the loft to find my husband lying prone in the front hallway, at a right angle to the stairs he has just descended at unintentional velocity. The cat he meant to carry down them is standing over him, with eyes shocked wide.

My own shock is trying to emerge as a volcanic giggling fit, but I manage to suppress it, just, and ask, 'Chris? Chris?'

He's breathing, thank God. He makes an answering noise. He's conscious.

Slowly, slowly, he pulls himself up into a sitting position. It's obvious that every little movement hurts, but he can move.

'Can you stand up?'

I help him to his feet.

'What happened?'

'I was carrying Beauchamp down to the kitchen, and when I slipped, my instinct was to grasp him tighter, like he was a baby, so I couldn't use my arms to break my fall. I think I've ripped all the skin off on one side – can you pull my shirt up and have a look for me?'

The skin's quite unbroken. When the GP comes the next day, she finds two cracked ribs and explains that the raw, burning sensation indicates torn connective tissue. It will mend, but slowly.

Too slowly. Some months from now, Chris will rub his left side and declare that if the pain doesn't stop, he'll kill himself, and I will scream at him to NEVER SAY THAT. NEVER SAY THAT AGAIN.

Julian had terrible, terrible back pain. It cost him hugely in medical bills, and lost him precious time at work.

**

When Chris and I decided to get married, the first thing I did was to email my brother with the news. He phoned as soon as he could, to tell us how delighted he was, to offer a thousand pounds towards our honeymoon as a wedding present, and to inform Chris that the going rate for Limburg women was two camels and a goat.

**

I felt so lucky to have found Chris. I never took it for granted that I would find anybody. Julian felt the same way. Along with our shared sense of humour came a shared sense of self-disgust.

I remember us having one of our heart-to-hearts, in my bedroom this time, I think, and I told him about an interview I'd seen with Peter Cook and Dudley Moore. When the interviewer asked Moore why he'd gone into therapy, he said that when he'd started, his self-esteem – or lack of it – was such that he was always astonished when everybody didn't vomit the minute he came into a room. As I'd expected, Julian gave the same ecstatic hoot of self-recognition that I'd made when I'd been watching Moore. I told my brother how I'd always assumed that if I ever dared to touch another person, they'd hit me, and be right to; he said he knew exactly what I meant, and felt the same.

**

The pain in Chris's side is suddenly worse, much worse. Bad enough for him to be quite transformed by it. He is slumped on the sofa, shuddering, a tear falling down his cheek. It's evening, so I call the out-of-hours service for him. A few hours later he returns from the clinic with a course of tramadol and the news that he has – probably – a kidney stone. Apparently the tramadol is amazing: you stop caring, about the pain or anything else, and then you go to sleep.

*
* *

I can't get to sleep. There's a noise in the room – a high-pitched tone, continuous and penetrating. I can't figure out where it's coming from. I go round the corner to check the equipment in my study, but the computer's off, the printer's off, the router's off, the speakers – it's all off. I go to the large window at the back of the house and listen there; sometimes the sounds of traffic on the A14 combine to produce a harmonic that makes it seem as if there's a ghostly machine hovering just over the playing fields behind the garden, humming gently. Not tonight, though; Chris can usually hear the humming ghost machine, but he can't hear this.

I throw myself irritably back into bed and lie down, as I usually do, on my left side. The noise grows louder. I roll over and push my right ear hard into the pillow. The noise gets quieter. I turn onto my back and the volume goes up again. This persecutory noise, it's coming neither from the office nor the A14, but from inside my ear. There are no cicadas to blame here. This is my noise and mine alone.

*
**

My mother can't stop coughing. It can tell it's a particularly vicious cough because it's painful even to hear. Sometimes I have to hold the telephone receiver a little away from my head when we're on the phone, to protect my eardrums from the jagged hack of it.

One of the specialists she's seeing – I can't remember which one, because they've been multiplying so much recently – diagnoses a post-nasal drip and prescribes a steroid spray, which gives her nosebleeds.

One day she calls from me Barnet General.

'Hello, darling (*cough*). More fun and games – I'm back at Barnet General. That bloody cough got worse again, and I went to the GP and she sent me here, just in case it was pneumonia. It is pneumonia. Again.'

'Oh no! Have they admitted you? I'll come down and visit.'

'No need (*cough*). They took a look at my chest just to be sure, and the X-ray was clear. I'm not breathless and my chest doesn't hurt, so they're sending me home. I'm just sitting here in Clinical Decisions – remember Clinical Decisions?'

'Yes.'

'Well it (*cough*) feels like my second home now, but I'm going home. I'm just waiting for my antibiotics and then they'll discharge me.'

'Ugh, I hate that part of it, that waiting at the end – it takes for ever.'

'Well it certainly feels like it does. I've got other places I'd rather be than here…'

'I know.'

My mother goes home and keeps coughing. She's expecting to go in for surgery on her parathyroid glands soon, but only if they think she's fit enough. Chris is grimacing, rubbing his side, waiting for his torn connections to knit; my limbs get heavier every day, and I'm bleeding more each month. Outside, a thick, early frost silvers the telephone pole, so it can send out glistening spiny tentacles to spread the cold from house to house.

**

'That's as bad as it gets,' says my therapist when I tell her about my airport dream.

I'm not sure whether to feel reassured or proud of myself.

'Do you know the New Testament at all?' she asks.

'I never did before, but I'm reading it at the moment – research for the Anne novel…'

'Have you heard of the Garden of Gethsemane?'

'That's where Jesus was captured.'

'That's right, but before he was captured he spent the night there, and it was the most terrible night for him; he prayed and he sweated blood, and his soul was "sorrowful *even unto death*" – even unto death. He knew what was coming, but he was desperate for a reprieve, and at the beginning of the night he prayed, "O my Father, if it be possible, let this cup pass from me", but the night went on and he watched, and he prayed, and before the morning came he prayed, instead, "O my Father, if this cup may not pass away from me, except I drink it, thy will be done."'

'That's beautiful.'

'Isn't it? But do you see what the point is?'

'That he came to an acceptance?'

'He came to an acceptance, but first he had to go through the worst night of his life, the night of watching and praying and sweating blood. We all come to a moment like this, and if we can only remain in it for long enough, no matter how much pain there is, how much fear, we can reach a place of peace that we never could have imagined… But now you look sceptical.'

I am sceptical, but I carry the image of Christ on his knees in the Garden around with me for the next few days, and because I imagine it as a beautiful picture, with the jewel-like colours of a medieval icon and a central figure delicately painted, looking up to heaven with enormous, misericord eyes, I can draw some kind of sustenance from it. I don't tell my mother about this; I'm not sure how she would feel about my deriving therapeutic benefit from the scriptures she wouldn't allow me to read at school. I don't tell her about the nightmare that provoked it either. In the last two years, I've got used to withholding most of my real thoughts and feelings from her. I've never told her that sometimes I torment myself by thinking of Julian's last months as his Stations of the Cross; or how I can't shake the conviction that we two survivors, our acts and omissions, are implicated in the story of his martyrdom.

.

And I wish that I could go back in time to tell my brother about the Garden of Gethsemane, and try to convince him that one can spend the night sweating blood, but still survive.

.

My mother's having tests. I'm having tests. It is as if I really have been sweating blood: my haemoglobin is down to 8.5, significantly below normal. I'm given iron supplements to take along with my antidepressants, thyroxin and gastro-resistant capsules; I consider buying a new pill-organizer. A pelvic ultrasound reveals the causes – nothing sinister, but I will need surgery.

An ENT surgeon takes a look inside my ear to see if he can find the source of the night-time tone. There's nothing obvious. He isn't worried but orders an MRI scan to be sure. While I'm waiting for the appointment, I learn about acoustic neuromas, benign tumours that sometimes grow on the nerve that runs from the brain to the ear. My mother has a tumour. Maybe I have a tumour?

On the day of the scan I am reading a medical history book in the waiting room, trying to understand how early modern people experienced their illnesses. He explains that, as they didn't have the sophisticated imaging that we take for granted now, the bodies they inhabited were in effect quite different from the bodies we inhabit today. We feel ourselves to have cells and hormones, antibodies, neural impulses; they felt the effects of excesses of blood or bile, of noxious vapours arising from their organs, of God talking to them through their flesh, chastising them for their sins with pains or fevers.

Today God chastises me by making the injection of the contrast dye into my arm particularly painful. He shows his mercy by lending me the grace to remain quite calm in the scanner. The grinding and knocking that comes out of the machinery doesn't bother me; I know what it is, that it will remain outside me, and do me no harm.

***

The ENT surgeon sends Mum for a scan. When the results come back they show not only the expected parathyroid adenoma, but also a 4.5cm mass in her right chest. The radiologist's opinion is that this is a lung tumour, either a primary in its own right or a secondary related to the breast cancer my mother had almost thirty years before.

I would have been twelve, or maybe thirteen, when I heard the news about the first cancer. My mother told me when she came back from the biopsy I hadn't known she was having. She was lying on her bed, in shock and still groggy from the anaesthetic. She didn't seem like herself in that moment, and the cancer didn't seem real. It never occurred to me at the time that what she had was life-threatening; she had a mastectomy, a lymphectomy and a course of radiation therapy, and of course it was horrible, but through all the months of her treatment and convalescence I don't think it occurred to me even once that we might lose her. Five years later, when I was eighteen, we were talking about it at the breakfast table when the realization finally caught up with me, and I burst into tears.

This time I get it straight away. I look up the survival rates for the lung cancer and they confirm what I already suspect: that there will be an end point to this story, of me, my mother and our tangled grief, and it will come unexpectedly soon. I remember how not so many months ago I had told my therapist that I wished my mother dead. I can't deny that I meant it, but I can't believe that I meant this. Not that she should suffer – only that I might somehow bargain with her life to get Julian's back, or, if that wasn't possible, to get her just to leave me alone – finally, for good.

And then I realize I'd known that this would happen, known that a sacrifice would be paid, that lung and breath and voice would be stripped out of the chosen victim, and that, once again, that victim wouldn't be me. The truth is, I'm not good or pure enough to be the sacrifice: mixed in with my horror, and my sadness, is the relief that there will be an end to all this.

I feel sick. I don't want to drink a pint of lung. But it's too late now; my cup will not pass from me, or my mother's cup from her, except we drink them. No cup-swapping allowed.

*
**

Alongside the medical history, I'm reading a book called *Silent Grief: Living in the Wake of Suicide*, by Christoper Lukas and

Henry M Seiden. Of the few books I've been able to find on the subject, it has been by far the most helpful to me. I'm learning about myself from it. For example, I'm learning that people in my situation make 'bargains', little arrangements with themselves and with their lives that enable them to carry on living with the unbearable fact of their 'survivorship'.

There are different kinds of bargains: some people choose to spend years saying goodbye, renouncing any kind of forward movement in their lives; some take the whole burden of guilt upon themselves and hang on to it; some find a scapegoat and blame them; some decide not allow themselves any kind of pleasure or happiness ever again; some keep running, making sure that they never stay long enough in any job or relationship to reach a point of stillness in which they would have to confront their grief; saddest of all are the bargains which require the grieving person's own death.

Of course I recognize myself: my guilt, my determination to hang on to sadness, my sneaking belief that it is against the just order of things for me to have any life left to me when my brother has none. But most of all I recognize that I have been scapegoating my mother, and that if I do not put aside my anger towards her, I run the risk of it destroying the little time we have left.

Vessel Nine

Q: After a parent dies, we recite the mourner's Kaddish
for them every day for eleven months, but after the
loss of a sister, brother, son, daughter or spouse,
we recite Kaddish for only thirty days. Why is the
mourning period for a parent so much longer?

A: *The Fifth Commandment tells us to honour our fathers and
mothers, who brought us into the world. By reciting Kaddish at
every service for this extended period, we honour them as we
should. It is also true that while it is quite possible to have more
than one sibling, child or (serially) spouse, the relationship a
person has with her mother or her father will be the only one of
its kind in her life.*

**

Another beach, another phone call. I am on the North Norfolk
coast. The tide is in, so I'm perched on what's left of the beach,
a steep and grudging pebble bank. We have just arrived in
Sheringham today, we are on our Easter break, and I mean to sit
on the beach, no matter how uncomfortable it is.

This time I phone her.

'Hello, darling.'

'Hi. Just wanted to tell you we've arrived.'

'Oh good. Enjoy. How are you finding it? How's the weather?'

'It's been beautiful, but there's a mist coming over. I've never seen one so thick, it's like someone's taking an eraser to the edge of the world... Anyway, how are you?'

'They phoned me with the biopsy results.'

'And?'

'It is lung cancer.'

'I'm sorry.'

'Well, I can't say it's a surprise.'

'I know but... What's next?'

'Another appointment with the lung specialist, and then the oncologist. Will you come with me?'

Yes. Of course I will.

**

I arrive at Mum's flat and the first thing we do is to go out to Tesco's to buy supper and some A4 plastic wallets. She drives us the short distance under a rust-coloured sky, and just as we park there is a great clap of thunder. No rain yet. When we get to the check-out, the man waiting in front of us is swearing loudly into his phone, about nothing very much.

Back at the flat, we get to work. Mum empties her desk of its papers. We agree that I should decide on the headings for the new filing system, as I will be the one retrieving the contents. So I take a few sheets of plain A4 and write in capital letters, one title for each sheet:

FINANCE/INCOME

FLAT – MAINTENANCE

UTILITIES/PHONE etc.

FLAT – PURCHASE AND DEEDS

INSURANCE

WILL

MEDICAL

CONTACTS AND ADDRESSES

Mum reminds me that when I need the number for the Jewish Joint Burial Society, all I'll need to do is look up the website of her synagogue and they'll have it there. Then we put all the filed papers back in the desk and talk about something else. Not Julian, though. Not yet.

⁂

Mum has her appointment with the lung specialist today, and I have arranged to meet her at the Royal Free. I arrive at Belsize Park far too early, so I go into a café, where I pick up an email from my sister-in-law. I have told her, via an intermediary, about my mother's condition. Now she sends her good wishes and promises to share some photographs of Giselle.

So I have some good news for my mother when I meet her in the lobby, and the prospect of the much-longed-for photographs does seem to buoy her up a bit. As we sit waiting outside the consulting room I bite down hard on my thumbnail and she laughs at me: 'You might need that thumb, you know!'

The lung specialist's door opens and we are ushered in to a tiny office. There are four of us in there – Mum, me, the specialist and the oncology nurse who looks after the lung-cancer patients – and we are almost knee to knee.

Everyone is introduced. The specialist starts – as all these appointments will start – by asking my mother what she understands about her condition so far. She gives a lucid answer. He nods and takes out the notes from her biopsy. The cancer in my mother's lung has metastasized to her sacrum and possibly also her liver, so it is quite definitely inoperable.

'So what's the prognosis?' Mum asks.

They can't talk about that: there are so many unknowns, as always. The useful question to consider is not how long, but what treatment. If the tissue taken during my mother's biopsy tests positive for the presence of a particular protein, then the first-line treatment will be administered as part of a research trial into a new drug. This would be a tablet taken at home that targets that protein directly and could switch off the instructions that are telling the cancer to grow.

'And if that's not possible?'

Then the first-line treatment will be chemotherapy – no, not the kind that completely lays waste to the patient, that is only given when the cancer is thought to be curable; this would be of the milder, palliative kind. But yes, it will compromise her immune system and have other side effects.

They make it clear that Mum doesn't have to undergo the chemo at all; some patients in her situation choose not to.

Mum and I look at each other. 'It's up to you,' I say. 'Whatever you want.'

'What do you recommend?' she asks.

The specialist says it's her decision. Some people decide, well I've had a good life, my priority now is to be comfortable for as long as possible and to use the time to do the things I most want to do, enjoy my family...

'I don't think I'm quite there yet,' Mum says.

So, treatment then?

'Yes.'

Then he'll refer her to the oncologist. They have had some success with the chemo, but it's not guaranteed: in one third of patients, the tumour shrinks; in another third, the growth is arrested; in the remaining third, the growth continues.

'I'll take those odds.'

OK. Any questions before the doctor has to go?

'Yes. I keep having this feeling of heaviness – I can't walk any kind of distance any more – is that from the cancer?'

Yes, that will be an effect of the toxins produced by the cancer cells; likewise, in all probability, her frequent evening fevers. He hopes that the treatment will bring some relief from all of these symptoms. He wishes her well.

The nurse stays with us a little longer, to explain the treatment in more detail and to hand us some information sheets on the treatment options. They are long and detailed, and we will need to read them tonight because she is going to add my mother to the end of the list for tomorrow's oncology clinic. We can ask more questions tomorrow.

I'm the one who asks for tissues. Mum keeps her strong face on and asks if she should get her affairs in order now. The nurse says yes, we advise people to do first what they have to do, and then what they want to do. As she says this, I notice that my mother has a foundation tidemark on her scalp. In the past I would have noted this detail and then forgotten about it, as make-up has never interested me, but for the first time in my life it occurs to me that Mum would want to know, that it would be helpful to tell her that she needs a lighter shade. It then occurs to me that on all the occasions when my mother annoyed me by pulling my hair out of my coat collar or pointing out the ladders in my tights, she might have genuinely meant to be helpful; she did these things because she would want someone else to do them for her. Suddenly, at the age of forty-one, I have a whole new way of thinking about our mother.

**

If only I could have figured this out before Julian died, and shared

my new Theory of Mum with him. My attempts to explain her
behaviour might have failed before, but maybe that was because
I lacked this vital proof of her good intentions.

It used to be that Julian explained Mum to me. He got her
measure, as he did most people's, many years before I did. I
remember complaining to him one day about Mum's going on
and on about some career option I was thinking about.

'She's driving me nuts – have I looked into this yet, have I sent
off for that, have I thought of talking to so-and-so…'

From across the Atlantic, I heard my brother sigh.

'Joanne, Joanne – have you not learned yet? Never on any
account apprise our mother of the vaguest desire to do anything.'

'I suppose she does always do this.'

'Yeah, she does. She does it with everything. Like, even if you
told her you were going to wash your bum, she'd be going on
and on saying, "Have you washed your bum yet? I think it would
be really good if you washed your bum. Have you thought about
washing your bum with this new soap I bought? You know so-
and-so's a bum-washing expert – why don't you have a chat to
them about it…?"'

He was right: Mum did do that with everything. She did it
with things we'd thought of, and she did it with things she'd
come up with herself. A few years after Mum's death, when
Ayako and I were making our first tentative steps towards
each other, I would ask her if she knew why my brother had
borrowed that blasted £20,000. She told me that as Julian's state

of mind worsened, he spent more and more, partly to make himself feel better, but also to compensate Ayako and Giselle for what he believed were his inadequacies as a husband and father. But this wasn't the whole story: he had needed at least some of the money to pay for a fence to go around their huge back garden. It was not the usual practice to fence gardens in their part of Plainsville, but to Mum the combination of a small child and a fenceless garden presented an unconscionable risk, and so, every time she phoned, she would go on and on about the fence. When Julian pointed out the prohibitive cost of fencing a garden of that size, she offered to lend him the money. So he took it, and fenced the garden, and that was one less thing for Mum to drive him mad about.

***

Mum and I have been told to arrive at oncology at half three, no earlier, and to expect a wait. Until then, the day must be spent somehow. We are very slow to move, and when the woman from the flat next door knocks to ask after my mother, we are both of us still wrapped in towels. I answer the door and say, yes, Mum does have lung cancer, I'm afraid, and that we're going to see the oncologist later today.

'Tell your mother "stem cells",' says the neighbour. 'They'll do the job. Someone I know had cancer – bad cancer – all over her body. They gave her donor stem cells and it cleared it all up.'

'That's wonderful,' I say, 'but it sounds like she probably had a blood cancer and was given donor marrow… but then you never know… I'll pass your good wishes on.'

We decide to have breakfast in the Italian deli across the road, and on the way we run into another neighbour, who is tending to the shrubs out in front of the building. She exclaims at the resemblance between Mum and me – it's uncanny!

'Are you alike in personality too?' she asks. In perfect unison, we say no! Then the neighbour shows us what she's been doing this morning: she's been planting a pair of clematis plants at the base of a dead lilac; by next year they will have grown and intertwined and the dead tree will be covered in blooms again.

'I haven't been able to work since I got ME,' she says, 'but this garden is my joy. It's my mission in life.'

After breakfast, Mum takes me to the newsagent's to buy me an Oyster Card, so that when I come down to help over the months to come, I can do so more cheaply. The shopkeeper looks from me to Mum and back again. Then he smiles broadly: 'Mummy…?'

**

It turns out that Mum is grateful to be told that she needs a different shade of foundation. She suggests that we take a bus to Brent Cross, where we visit the Clinique counter at Fenwick's. Mum finds her perfect shade while I spend too much on skincare products, because my face seems all of a sudden to be ageing rapidly. Then we go into Banana Republic and I try on two T-shirts, which Mum insists on buying. These will turn out to be the last things she ever buys for me and I will hang on to them long after they have ceased to be wearable.

We have lunch in Carluccio's. Then we take the C11 to the Royal Free.

'It's going to take you past your childhood,' Mum says, and yes, we turn left by the Brent Cross flyover, go past Clitterhouse Park which still has so much grass for running on and such a good set of swings, past the end of Pennine Drive where my father's parents and my mother's mother used to catch the bus to Cricklewood or Golders Green, and then past the end of Cheviot Gardens where we ate so many fondant fancies and so much cauliflower, overboiled.

The nurse was quite right to warn us about the wait. We spend two hours in the waiting area oncology shares with cardiology, which is plenty of time to take in the rows of seats and the thinness and pallor of their occupants. Men outnumber women, and I wonder if one of today's oncology clinics is for patients with brain tumours, because most of the men seen to have shaven areas on their heads with what look like newly healed holes in the middle. Many of the men are with their wives, who spend the time talking over the broken, silent heads of their husbands, comparing treatments with each other, discussing arrangements with the nurses, and all of this in the brisk tone that women use to complain that their husbands have bought the wrong colour of lavatory paper, or forgotten that the Smiths were coming to dinner. I recognize it: it's the coping tone, it means that this can be coped with.

There is one man, not old, who is sitting by himself, his walking frame propped in front of him. A nurse sits down next to him and explains his medication to him: take this many pills at this time for chemo, then that many of the anti-nausea pills – no, those are the chemo, you take this many of them, that many of the others – no, you take these before those – no, these are the anti-nausea pills, and you take so many... After the third repetition, he says he's got it, but I'm not convinced. I think he's just trying to save face; I imagine the nurse must know that too. He keeps making little jokes as they help him into his wheelchair and push him away.

There is a glassed-in area next to reception, where Macmillan volunteers can give information and advice, or just listen. I go in and ask if they have anything to help me explain cancer to children, because my son is going to notice something soon. The volunteer is very kind. She keeps insisting I sit down, which I'm sure I don't need to do just now.

At last the seats clear and we are called. We are met by the registrar Dr Y., and the consultant, Dr B., who has come at the end of her clinic to sit in until, she explains, she will have to leave for a meeting. Later Mum will tell me that – like me – she has noticed Dr B.'s Prada handbag and taken it as a sign of success in the cancer-fighting business.

Dr Y. asks Mum to explain back to them what she understands from yesterday's meeting and is impressed by the fullness and accuracy of the answer. The two doctors go over the scan results in more depth, explaining that the lesion on Mum's liver did not show up on one particularly crucial image and is therefore 'neither here nor there'. They go through the consent process for the experimental treatment. They then take a very detailed medical and social history – including the whole story of my brother – and as they do so they speak to us in such a way as to suggest that they are expecting this to be a longish and close-ish relationship – something I find both reassuring and chilling.

I ask if Mum will need me to stay and nurse her during the chemo, if that is what she has. They say she won't; it will be the lower, non-curative dose, and won't prevent her from looking after herself. Mum asks if she will be able to have her hair coloured if she has the chemo and they explain that she won't, as the hair will be too brittle. Mum says she hates going grey and looking old.

Then Dr Y. performs a quick examination and says the signs are hopeful: she cannot find any fluid on the lungs, and as for the fevers, they could just as well be caused by my mother's hypercalcaemia as by her cancer. Dr B. asks about my mother's liver function: has she ever had jaundice?

'Just once,' Mum says. 'The only time I ever went yellow was when I was twenty-four and my doctor put me on Largactil. But I came off it straight away – it knocked me out too much as well as turning me a funny colour.'

I'm astonished; I know that Largactil is a psychiatric drug and Mum has always told me that she never needed any until our father died. The doctors look taken aback too, and it is Dr B. who asks the question: why?

'Oh, I'd just had a bad break-up with a boyfriend,' Mum says. 'I was a bit low, that's all.'

Dr B. has to go. The nurse joins us, and hands over still more information: booklets about support and services, and how we might be feeling. One way or another, the treatment will begin very soon.

**

It's getting on for two months since my mother's diagnosis, one month since our visit to the oncologist, and I'm disturbed by how little I've cried so far. I do want to, but I can't. Even when I attend a local support-group meeting for people bereaved by suicide and talk about my brother for two solid hours, I can only shed a token tear. The discomfort is physical, as if I really do have all that salty fluid banking up behind my uptight ducts.

I've got a hospital appointment of my own today. My MRI was clear, so I have been to see a specialist clinical psychologist to receive advice on managing tinnitus, and at 9.30 this morning I have my follow-up. There really isn't much to discuss. I return the white-noise machine which I haven't found helpful and say that, actually, I feel that I've accepted my tinnitus, which is mild really. Compared to what's happening with my mother it seems quite trivial.

The psychologist has a quiet, deliberate, restrained sort of voice, not the kind of voice anyone acquires by accident, and his words, too, are carefully chosen. In his gentle, euphemistic way, he tells me that many people who are on the kind of journey I have begun with my mother may well feel that their tinnitus seems trivial by comparison, but also warns that I may find, when the journey reaches its destination, that my tinnitus will, temporarily, become much worse. He wants to assure me that if it does, I can always come back.

So, leaving his metaphorical door open, I close his literal one behind me and walk back out into the foyer, thinking, journey… destination… and a song starts playing in my head.

I'm just a poor wayfaring stranger

Travellin' through this world of woe…

I should be turning right towards the outpatients' lobby and the bus stop, but I find myself hesitating.

There's no sickness, toil nor danger

In that fair land to which I go…

I make a decision, and turn right.

I'm going home to see my father

I'm going home no more to roam…

I set off down the first of several long, long corridors at a quick march, in step with the busy people in scrubs, overtaking shuffling people in tears, easily passing the people on trolleys, who can neither march nor shuffle down the corridors, but without help can only furnish them.

I'm just a-going over Jordan

I'm just a-going over home…

I turn right again, and carry on across the main concourse, past Costa, past the gift shop, past the pale-skinned, bald child whose parents are wheeling him to Burger King.

I'm going there to meet my mother

She said she'd meet me when I come…

When I reach the chapel, I take a left.

I'm going home to see my brother,

I'm going there no more to roam…

Here's the Cancer Support Centre. I've walked past it many times, but this morning it's my turn to go in. I need to sit down now, because I'm going to cry.

⁎

In May I travel to Birmingham to attend a support day run by an organization called Survivors of Bereavement by Suicide. On arrival I am given a blue name badge: a blue badge signifies a lost sibling, pink a lost partner, white a lost child. There are plenary sessions in the morning. After lunch we split up into groups; I join the smallest of these, which is for the blue-badge holders, the siblings. The group facilitator is a founder member of the organization, who has lost a son. A man who works with the police to support bereaved families is also joining us, with our consent. The rest of us are here because we have lost brothers – or, in one case, a sister. I have read that, statistically speaking, men are far more at risk of 'completing' suicide, and the people I meet at the support day bear this out: for most of the time, we are talking about sons, brothers, fathers, boyfriends, husbands. (*The Lord hath trodden under foot all my mighty men in the midst of me…*)

The tears begin with the introductions. First to speak is a woman who lost her brother only two months ago, who says she doesn't really feel well enough to join in but will not be able to stop herself from speaking all the way through the session; she is at the Ancient Mariner stage of grief, when the words come out in torrents. One very young woman bursts into tears as soon as it is her turn to speak, and the tissue box sitting in the middle of the circle has to be pushed in her direction so that she can sort herself out. She will say nothing more after her introduction, but later will nod vigorously when I say how much I hate it when people say that suicide is selfish, that while it is true that my brother was overwhelmed by his own internal world, his motives in doing what he did could not be called selfish – selfish is a different creature altogether.

The facilitator opens the discussion with a short speech, explaining that as siblings we are often called 'the forgotten mourners'. As she says this, I wonder if the reason why our group is so small is that many of us wonder if we even have the right to see ourselves as wounded, compared to the parents, partners and children, the scale of whose loss is so clear to everyone who hears of it.

Another heartbreakingly young woman has a question: did anyone's sibling leave a note? The woman sitting next to me, who has professional as well as personal experience in this area, says that people often think that a note, in the absence of one, would explain things. In practice they never do, or at least only rarely. I tell the group that my brother's certainly hadn't explained anything, that it was mostly about the financial arrangements. I have read a book by the suicidologist, Edwin Shneidman, and have learned that this was typical of the genre.

There are other stories, stories of police searches and dragged rivers, discussed with the police worker in the kind of detail you might expect from a forensic specialist, and I find myself thinking about how the situation we've all been through has turned us into lay experts in areas we would never otherwise have thought, or wanted, to explore. There are stories of regret, of 'if onlys', of clues and opportunities missed. We each have our collection of these, little shards to squeeze in our hands until we bleed, and it doesn't matter how many times we are told that we couldn't have stopped it, we are compelled to clutch them, and to cut ourselves, perhaps until the day they wear down from ceaseless handling. I tell the group, at some length, about the problems my brother was having at work. The woman next to me repeats that, no matter how many times I comb every bit of information, I'll still never know why. The search for answers is a symptom of suicide bereavement, not its solution.

Then there are stories about anger – anger at parents and the guilt that comes in its train. I say that I did feel angry with my mother, but add that since her diagnosis we have gone some way to sorting it out. I talk about the book I read that had helped me to realize what I was doing with the anger, that to feel it was a way of keeping my brother close. I say I'm not sure whose anger it was I was feeling: mine or my brother's. The facilitator says we are often not nice people when we are mourning a suicide; sometimes we can feel quite murderous.

Of all the stories of loss I hear, the woman's next to me seems nearest to mine. Her brother was not her only sibling, but he was her closest, and younger. I tell the group about a dream I had: I was talking normally to my brother one moment, just bantering on the phone as usual, when suddenly the mood of the dream darkened and I felt compelled to ask him why he did it, but he couldn't tell me. All he could say was, he didn't know, he got distracted… She nods all the way through, and then recounts an almost identical dream. It is this, more than anything else I hear at the meeting, which helps me to feel slightly less alone.

**

My mother's cancer is not the kind that would respond to the experimental drug, so she is to begin her first cycle of chemo in late June. I tell her that I will come down and sit with her during the infusion. I think that if I do this – sit with her and stay with her when my full emotional presence might help her most – I might somehow make up for some of the time and energy I have spent since Julian's death in denying her that presence.

I'm not to be allowed this bargain, though. Mum is told that there is no space – literally no space – for relatives in chemotherapy. And in the event, on the day when she eventually goes in for her first treatment (there are delays, there are mix-ups), I am myself in hospital in Cambridge, undergoing minor surgery on my middle-aged womb. Mum has to receive her medical poison alone, without her daughter there, and I have to go on ageing alone, without my brother.

**

Mum calls me on my mobile at 7.40 in the morning, when I've just finished making my son's lunch, and am listening to the *Today* programme, drinking the coffee that I hope will wake me up.

She tells me she's in hospital. She reminds me that it's about ten days since her first chemo treatment, and that the oncologist did warn her that this would be her immune system's lowest point. When she took her temperature last night it was very high, so she did what she was supposed to do and took herself to the Royal Free. Now she is in the oncology ward, getting her intravenous antibiotics.

When I put the phone down I'm ambushed by another crying fit. I'm supposed to go to my son's sports day, but I decide that Mum needs me more. He says he understands, and I praise him for being so grown-up.

On the way up from Belsize Park I buy some flowers – I know Mum appreciates flowers – but when I get to the door of the ward, the first thing I see is a notice explaining that the patients behind it are immunocompromised and therefore no flowers are allowed. I am left standing on the eleventh-floor lobby with a huge bouquet that I have to lose before I can visit my mother. I cross the lobby and go into the opposite ward, which does not appear to have an embargo on flowers. I look for a nurse or health assistant to give them to but find nobody. After a few minutes' hesitation, I decide to leave them on a counter in an empty sluice room and make my escape.

I find my mother in a four-bed room, which she shares with one other patient and a heap of broken furniture. She is attached to a drip but otherwise her usual self, ready to express herself forcibly on all her usual subjects, familial, social and political, to me and then her brother and sister-in-law, for hours. By the time I have to go, at ten to six, she is detached from the drip, and waiting for the oncologist.

I spend a minute or two listening to the wind wailing down the half-dozen lift shafts, then take the first that arrives. Two floors down, I'm joined by a couple of elderly men in surgical gowns. One has a packet of cigarettes in his hand. He'll be going down to the entrance to smoke. Every hospital has its cluster of smokers, some attached to drips, posted like guards at the doors.

Standing behind the smoking man, I am unable not to see the giant plaster he wears on the back of his head. A drain comes out of it: as I follow it with my eyes, it goes down his back, curves back on itself a little way and then disappears underneath his gown; in the bend of the tube there is a tiny, stagnant pool of blood. When I get out of the lift I hurry round a corner so as not to be seen and then retch. I'd never make a nurse.

Mum phones me again in the evening, to report on her visit from the oncologist.

'I told her I was already coughing less, and she said that it can sometimes happen that quickly. I'm waiting to be discharged now, and then I'll be back in again next week to have a permanent line put into my arm, and then they'll use that for the second lot of chemo.'

'So it's worth carrying on with it?'

'Oh yes, but I do wonder if this is going to be a pattern for all the treatments: chemo then infection then hospital...'

'And if it is?'

'If it is, I'll think again.'

⁎

13 July: Mum calls from hospital again. She was supposed to be receiving her second treatment tomorrow, but she won't be well enough. She's been a bit confused, dizzy and missing words, so the doctors have ordered an emergency CT scan, but I shouldn't worry too much: her blood sugar level is elevated, as it can be with chemo, and this may be sufficient to account for the confusion.

And what else…? Oh yes: they can't get a line into her arm, so she'll have to have a port in her chest from now on. On the plus side, the lesion on her lung – the tumour – seems to have shrunk already…

⁎

I travel down to London to visit Queen Anne in the British Library, and Mum in her flat. Anne is needy, and continually pregnant; Mum is thin, still coughing – though she says she is coughing less than before – and unable to hear the doorbell while we are talking. The chemo is eating away at her hearing, and she won't get it back. But she has been able to get herself to Waitrose, and insists on preparing dinner.

'Are you OK with us going to Vienna this week?' I ask.

'Of course I am! You have to have a holiday! You're recovering from your own surgery! Go and enjoy yourself!'

So we fly to Vienna, the three of us; we take the boy to the zoo
and the aquarium; he trails round the art galleries with us; we eat
far too much cake and ice cream, and in the evenings, we sit in our
borrowed flat and watch London burn.

'Tory blight,' Chris says. 'There are always riots under the
Tories.'

There are no riots in Finchley, but I phone Mum; I would have
phoned her anyway.

'I'm all right, darling,' she says. 'It's very good of you to phone
– it's going to be ever such an expensive call for you.'

Does she have to mention money?

⁎⁎

On 14 August 2011, I open up a Word document and head it
'Three Fucking Years Ago'. I write:

> Mum has just had her third chemo, so is halfway through
> the course of six. For the first two treatments, she was given
> cisplatin, which made her feel extremely ill, left her with an
> infection after the first treatment and has damaged her hearing
> – maybe permanently, but they won't know for a year yet. The
> other day when I was on the phone to her, I heard her front
> doorbell and she didn't.

They've switched to another platinum-based drug, and she is
feeling far better this time. The tumour in her lung has already
begun to shrink, as far as they can tell from X-rays, and she is

coughing far, far less. When she phoned me yesterday, she was Mum-as-usual, venting about something she'd read in the *Guardian*, speaking to me as Gladstone would speak to Queen Victoria, as if addressing a public meeting. This in turn brought out Joanne-as-usual, who is far too quickly irritated.

'I know, I know, I know, yeah, yeah, yeah it is wicked...' I drawled.

She gave a little laugh. 'OK, your mother's a *big bore*.'

'I didn't say that. It's just that I'm not a public meeting, Mum.'

'No, and I'm not Gladstone.'

I apologize. She's not Gladstone, her clothes are hanging off her and only three years ago she lost her son. If he were here today I could phone him and we could commiserate about how our mother still goes *on and on* and in the process *drives us mad*, but since that day three fucking years ago, there's been no us, to commiserate or giggle or even to fight.

⁂

Although they have switched Mum to a different chemo drug, the cisplatin has remained in her body and still does her harm. This week it attacked her bone marrow and she had to have four units of blood. She is weaker every day, but she says there's no need for me to come down.

But when my cousin visits my mother, she is shocked by the state she's in; she phones me to ask if I've spoken to the clinical nurse specialist about Mum. So I phone the clinical nurse specialist and she reassures me that my mum is not so ill as to need a nurse full-time. I phone the Macmillan helpline to offload my confusion. Mum continues to phone me every day. Sometimes we have our usual, ritual exchanges: she tells me everything she's done that day and wants to know everything I've done, and then she vents about what she's read in the *Guardian*. When we have those conversations, I feel all the stubborn old feelings, the irritation, impatience and guilt, but more and more often there are moments when we pause, and all the interference quiets, and we can talk to each other in the present, about what is really going on in it.

'You know, I had to have a rest after my shower this morning. It's ridiculous, isn't it?'

'You always say that, but in the context, it's not ridiculous at all... Is it... is it that you *want* it to be ridiculous?'

'Yes. I just want to feel well. Sometimes I think I'll never feel entirely well again. I guess if that happens I'll just have to adjust my expectations.'

⁎

We have reached September, and the altitude of the oncology ward at the Royal Free must have cleared our heads, because for the first time since Julian died, Mum and I talk honestly about him, about our childhoods, about the upbringing that she gave us, and what he said to me about it.

'And what do you think? Do you think I emotionally abused you?'

'No! No, I don't – but *you* were, weren't you? Your brother said so.'

'Yes. My aunts were bitches to me – absolute bitches.'

'I've thought about it, I've thought about it a lot, and… I think there are emotional inheritances in families, and I think that when a child's constantly criticized like you were, you want to do everything to protect yourself from it, and you protect yourself from it by trying never ever to make a mistake that someone might get you for. And I've realized, only lately, that maybe all the times I've thought you were nagging me – about my appearance, or my job, or whether I was going out enough – you were trying to protect me from criticism from internalized aunts – does that sound stupid?'

'No, not stupid at all – though I would suggest some of them weren't even internalized.'

'Yetta?'

'Yetta.' We laugh, and I tell her the story about Yetta telling Julian that he was fine and me that I was *funny.* The mention of Julian makes us quiet again.

'You know,' I say, 'I was angry with you after Julian died.'

'I know. I was angry with you too.'

And that's all we say on that subject. It's all that's needed.

*
**

The day after my visit is a Monday, and Mum is discharged. She phones in some distress to tell me that someone has defrauded her by cheque and to ask me how much shit one person can take. I tell her how sorry I am, and that one should never, ever ask that question. She phones on Tuesday morning to tell me that she has sorted the problem with the bank. That evening she phones again, from an ambulance, to let me know that she has broken her hip.

'I just turned to pick something up and fell down and it broke – they think maybe the cisplatin damaged my balance as well as the hearing.'

On Thursday she has an operation on the hip, which goes well. On Friday, the physios visit. They get her sitting up on the bed and then standing with a frame. They consider helping her sit in a chair, but decide that she's had enough for one day. In Cambridge, I arrange to meet a friend at the Boden end-of-line sale at the Guildhall. We both need cheering up, and the purchase of clothes we couldn't usually afford might help.

'But don't they all look miserable?' my friend whispers. There is a typical Boden Sale Woman, we have discovered: thin, well-dressed and exquisitely groomed, she marches efficiently from table to table, raking through piles of discounted tunics in a manner as joyless as it is methodical.

'They often do, though, don't they?' I hiss back. 'The rich wives.'

'Perhaps we should take a moral from this,' my friend says. 'You might think that more money would make you happy, but actually you'd just never be able to enjoy anything any more.'

'Absolutely. We're so lucky we're not *them.*'

'Oh *so* lucky.'

My friend finds a straight, knee-length skirt and is delighted with it. I find a lightweight fitted cardigan the colour of the Mediterranean in early summer, and am very pleased. I decide to look for something for my mother.

'We're taking the boy to visit her on Sunday. He hasn't seen her all summer – I think it'll be a shock.'

'Does she look very ill?'

'She's lost a lot of weight, her skin's grey – and something big has changed, since the fall. I think it's been a real shock to the system – her voice sounds weaker on the phone… She's supposed to be discharged next week and I've said I'll look after her in the flat, and of course I will, but to tell you the truth I'm really scared. What if I drop her and she gets injured again? What if—'

My phone goes and it's my mother. There's been a change of plan – she's to be discharged to a rehabilitation unit a few streets away from her flat.

'To be honest,' I say, 'I think that's better. This way when you get back to the flat, I know you'll be recovered enough for me to really look after you properly…'

I wish immediately I hadn't said this, and change the subject. 'I'm at a Boden sale. I'm looking for a present for you – what would you like?'

'Ooh, you don't have to… How about a nice top? All my clothes are too big. Can you get a long-sleeved top? Size fourteen?'

I find her a nice scoop-necked top, in lilac. Mum and I say the wrong things to each other all the time, or fail to say the right things, but at least we can buy each other presents. I remember what my therapist said: *Money is never just money.*

**

Mum is cheered by the sight of her grandson, but he has never visited anyone in hospital before and is visibly shocked. Chris takes him out, supposedly to buy Mum the cheese straws she fancies from M&S, but really – so Chris tells me later – so that his dad can explain it all to him: why Grandma can't get out of bed; why she looks so thin; why there is a see-through box of yellow liquid attached to the bed; why all the people in the other beds are so old; why one of the old ladies keeps calling out for things but no one comes.

This old lady, in the opposite corner from my mother, is what people politely call 'confused'. Someone has given her a Sunday newspaper, still in its cellophane wrapping, and she seems to have forgotten that the wrapping can be easily torn. Every few minutes she makes scissoring motions with her hand and shouts: 'Has anyone got any SCISSORS?' You know – SCISSORS – for CUTTING.'

**

It's late on Tuesday afternoon and something feels wrong. I search back through my memory of the day to try and figure out what's missing and then I realize – it's late in the afternoon and Mum hasn't phoned me yet. So I phone her.

'Hello, darling!' She sounds surprised to hear from me, and also – sort of… wavery… *wrong*. 'It's nice of you to phone.'

'Why wouldn't I phone? I didn't hear from you today – I was worried… How was your first night in the new place?'

'Oh, OK… but I think I said yesterday, the next youngest patient has at least ten years on me… I don't think they're really set for… Oh Joanne, I had such a rude awakening this morning!'

'Why, what happened?'

'I woke up to find a hand in my bed! There was a nurse feeling about under me, and I asked her what she was doing and she barked at me, "I need to check if the bed's dry," and then off she went – without a by-your-leave!'

'That's *horrible*!'

'It's that kind of place. I've decided to find it funny.'

'Hmm…' I've decided to complain when I get there, but I don't mention it for now.

'And then I had a fright later. I suddenly got all breathless, couldn't breathe at all – they sprayed some medication down my throat and that made it better, but I was really frightened, I thought that was it!'

'I can imagine – but it wasn't.'

'No. I've put it behind me. I've been trying to read. Your uncle lent me Simon Sebag Montefiore's history of Jerusalem – have you heard of it?'

'Yes.'

'It's very good, but oh, I'm reading so slowly now. I've had it for days and I'm still only on page 177…'

'But you're still reading.'

'Oh yes, quite a heavy read though, maybe not the best for a rehab ward! Sandra's coming later with smoked-salmon sandwiches, she said, so I may ask her to fetch me something lighter.'

'Might be an idea.'

'Anyway, she'll be here soon – and you're coming on Thursday.'

'Yes.'

'I'm looking forward to it. It's lovely of you to phone me, darling.'

'Lovely of me to phone my own mother?'

'It's always lovely to hear from you. I'll see you on Thursday. Bye-bye, darling.'

'Bye, Mum.'

*
**

Wednesday. Five thirty in the morning. The landline wakes me.

'Is that Joanne Limburg? I'm phoning regarding your mother, Ruth Limburg. We found her at half one, she wasn't breathing, and we worked on her for a long time, but I'm afraid she passed – we're sorry for your loss, Ms Limburg, we're sorry for you…'

How doth the city sit solitary…

*
**

It isn't fair, any of it.

It isn't fair that I have to wake my eight-year-old son up at seven and tell him that Grandma Ruth is dead, and it isn't fair that he's lost her.

It isn't fair that I have to travel all the way to London to get to the rehab hospital just so they can hand me her rings, her watch, her washbag, the book still marked on page 177 and the Boden top she never wore, and then tell me that the Burial Society can't pick her up because she's already gone to the coroner's.

It isn't fair that when I phone the coroner and say that my mother is Jewish and that we need to bury her before Rosh Hashanah begins, they tell me that her body is the property of the Crown.

It isn't fair that it takes a whole day of phone calls to the coroner's office, the Burial Society, my uncle and the synagogue to get the authorities to recognize their statutory duty to be culturally sensitive and move the post-mortem forward so that I can bury my mother at the weekend.

It isn't fair that for hours nobody can tell me where my mother's body is and that when my cousins drive me at last to a funeral home in North Kensington to say goodbye to her that they have laid her out in a polyester shroud with a rose in her hands which is both so kitsch and un-Jewish that I am mortified on her behalf. Because it turns out that Jewish law does matter to me, when its violation affects my mother.

It isn't fair that I should be manoeuvred into writing another eulogy when I'm still in shock, because yet another rabbi never knew another loved one.

And it isn't fair – it really isn't fair – that I should have to do all of this without Julian; that when I walk behind the coffin at my mother's burial, I have only my Uncle Richard's hand to hold, and not my brother's.

And it isn't fair on Uncle Richard either, that he should have to survive his younger sibling. And it wasn't fair on him that he should have had to take that call, and be the first to hear about his nephew's suicide, and then have to phone his nephew's sister – his niece – and then deliver the news to his nephew's mother – his sister. The memory of all this will weigh on him for the rest of his life, and that really isn't fair.

But then, as my mother used to say:

'Who promised you life would be fair? NOT ME!'

*
*

Ruth was born Ruth Helen Savinson on 15 January 1937, the younger child and only daughter of Henry and Mary Savinson, on the Pennine Drive estate in Golders Green. Her early life was difficult: her father was killed in a road accident in 1941, her mother had to work and she was then evacuated to a children's home in Hemel Hempstead, where she spent two years. She then grew up in a house full of relatives, where there was little money to go around and even less privacy – when she had her own children later, she would make a point

of never going into their rooms without asking permission
first.

Despite all this, Ruth did well at school, moving from Wessex
Gardens Primary School to Copthall County Grammar to
Bristol University, where she read history and had a great,
aunt-free time. After graduating, she got a postgraduate
certificate in social sciences, before training as a medical
social worker, or – in the language of the time – 'lady
almoner'. She went on to have a long and successful career
in social work in various NHS hospitals, finishing up as head
of department at the North Middlesex, before moving into the
voluntary sector, where she was the first woman on the board
of directors at Jewish Care.* She never stopped working;
after she was officially retired, she had several jobs: as chair
of NHS complaints panels, as a counsellor and counselling
supervisor, as an inspector of postgraduate medical schools
and latterly as mentor to medical students in GP practices.

Long before *I Don't Know How She Does It* was ever thought
of, Ruth was a working mother. After a two-year stint working
in Israel, she came back to London and was thinking of
leaving again, this time for the States, when she met Maurice
Limburg at a party; although they had lived a few streets
apart their whole lives, this was the first time they had ever
seen each other. They married in 1967 and had two children:
Joanne, born in April 1970, and Julian, born in May 1972.
She was a loving and protective mother throughout her life,
and was fiercely proud of both her children, and later of her

---

*   A large Jewish voluntary organization.

grandchildren. She also retained at all times a very motherly interest in her nieces and nephews, in their children, in her friends' children, her children's friends, her children's friends' children and even her friends' children's children, and would knit or quilt for any of the above at the drop of a needle.

Alongside her working, mothering and needlework, Ruth had many other interests. She was a tireless voluntary worker, visiting Soviet Jews in the 1980s, and helping to found Jewish Women's Aid in the 1990s. She loved to travel, often with friends, and visited, among other places: Peru, China, the Southern United States, India and South Africa; she saw penguins in the Antarctic and polar bears in northern Canada. Her curiosity was cultural as well as geographical: she was always on her way to see whatever was new in the cinema, theatre, opera or ballet. She read books – especially murder mysteries – by the ton. She shared a love of science fiction with her husband, and was an enthusiastic and knowledgeable Trekkie.

What is clear from all this is that Ruth had a gift for getting the most out of life, something she was determined to do even in the face of illness and sorrow, of which she had more than her fair share. She survived breast cancer in her forties, then lost her beloved husband Maurice before they had a chance to share the retirement they had looked forward to. Her son Julian also predeceased her, in the most tragic circumstances, three years ago. His death hit her hard, of course, but she moved out of the family home in Stanmore to a flat in Finchley, where she rebuilt her life and almost immediately, in characteristic fashion, set about finding a better management company for the residents of her block.

Ruth was a problem-solver by nature, but she was also a realist, and when she received her diagnosis of lung cancer in April this year she faced it bravely, sorting out her affairs with her daughter before embarking on treatment. Although her death was unexpected in its timing, and a shock to many, in dying as she did – quickly and peacefully in her sleep – she went as most of us would wish to go, and was spared any further suffering. She will be fondly remembered by her daughter, her brother, her grandson, by her extended family, and by her many many friends.

There Is No Vessel Ten

Nor could there be, because *Keter*, the Crown, which is the highest of the *Sefirot*, is unknowable to human consciousness.

It is not for me to complete the work.

I cannot complete it because of the impossibility of remembering what really happened – hence the Midrashim, the made-up conversations.

I cannot complete it because the other main participants in the story – my mother, my brother – are gone, and they have taken their perspectives with them. Often in the writing I have had an impulse to ring either one and check a memory or a fact, only to realize…

I should not complete it because completion implies the closure of a case; the closure of a case implies the passing of judgement upon the parties involved, and it is not for me to judge anyone else in my family's story. Anyone else would have different fragments, and arrange them differently. Only G–d, if such a being exists, possesses them all, and can put them in their proper order.

It is not possible for me to complete the work. This arrangement of the fragments is provisional only. Tomorrow I will have to break it and start all over again.

*
*

It is not for us to complete the work; neither can we bring back what we have lost. According to 'Internet Rabbi' Daniel Kohn, the Temple can never be rebuilt. The religion described in the Torah, he explains, is 'not modern Judaism. The Torah describes an ancient biblical cult based on animal sacrifices at a temple administered by priests';[*] what Jews have practised since is a religion based not on the Torah itself, but on the rabbinical interpretations of it. Judaism has 'evolved into a non-sacrificial religion based on prayer and acts of charity'.[†] God no longer requires the slaughter of animals; what He wants is observance, on the one hand, and kindness, on the other.

*
*

Modern Judaism is not the religion of the woman who weeps in Lamentations, neither is any modern nation-state a polity or

---

[*]　Rabbi Daniel Kohn, *Jewish FAQs: An Internet Rabbi's Answers to Frequently Asked Questions about Judaism*, Amazon Kindle edition (Bloomington, Indiana: Xlibris, 2009).

[†]　Kohn, 'Chapter Eight, Answer number 25'.

society that she would recognize. She cannot in the fully literal sense go home, and neither can I. When my mother died, and the nuclear family of my birth was truly finished, I felt as if I had been abruptly discharged from some long-term institution where I had spent my entire life; I imagined myself standing outside the gates as they slammed shut behind me, standing with a holdall in each hand, wondering why this sudden freedom felt so much like emptiness.

⁎⁎

I had to sell my mother's flat. I had to clear it and decide which of its contents I could keep. For two years it had functioned as a kind of family *genizah*, a stay of disposal for various beloved objects. Now I had to consider how much room I had in my present life for the remnants of my old one. I kept the *Complete Dickens*; I kept the Georgette Heyers which I'd loved to read as an adolescent, and my mother's first edition of *Lord of the Rings*. Most of the other books, with their dear, familiar spines, I had to give away to Oxfam. Worse, I had to sell the Ercol dining set, which had hosted so many Shabbat dinners and Passover Seders, disappeared under so much sprawling homework and course work, even provided my brother and me with a serviceable ping-pong table. I had sat on every chair. I knew every scratch on the table's surface. I knew it from underneath, where the extra leaf was stored and the other two leaves were secured in place at the sides by wing nuts that looked like metal dragonflies; I must have crawled under it countless times. It was the wooden embodiment of the life I had shared with my father, mother and brother in our old house in Stanmore. I had no room for it now.

.*.

Mum would sometimes remind me that the word for Jewish law, *halakhah*, can be translated as 'the path I walk', or, as she used to say, 'the walk forward'. She wanted me to see that Judaism was inherently pragmatic and progressive, that it was designed to adapt itself to changing settings, changing times. In this spirit, our parents brought us up in the Reform movement: women and men sat together in synagogue; parts of the service were in English; by the time I was in my teens, some of the services were being led by female rabbis (I even – very briefly – thought about becoming one myself).

But my brother and I didn't just walk forward – we ran, we ran like the clappers. The distance my brother ran was evident – expressed, as it was, geographically. I have also run a very long way, but it takes my son to show me just how far.

My novel is published in the summer of 2015. The *Jewish Chronicle* prints a favourable review, and sends someone out to interview me. Naturally it's not only Queen Anne's Protestantism they want to discuss. I don't mind; I'm well into the writing of this – very Jewish – book by now.

We talk about Jewishness, Judaism, ancestors and family. When the article appears, I read myself explaining how 'My mother, my family and Judaism are nested inside each other. I am Jewish and always Jewish; it's analogous with family; however hard it is, and however strained, it can never be disavowed.'

There is a shorter, punchier version of this statement printed in red, as a pull quote:

'I am Jewish,

always Jewish.

However hard

or strained, it

can never be

disavowed.'

I show my twelve-year-old son the article, and he points to the quote.

'Is that true?' he asks. 'Did you really say that? Is that really what you think?'

'Yes,' I say. Then, with a cheerful expression and absolutely no malice at all, he says, 'Well, I guess that ends with me!'

The mothers, the family members, the Jewish ancestors that nest inside me start in horror. I can hear their agitated voices: *You might as well remember that you're Jewish – 'cause if you don't, the Anti-Semites will remind you... If you don't raise Jewish children, you're letting Hitler win... He's Jewish whatever, because it comes from the mother – it's not up to him! It's not up to you!*

I feel all their shock, all their sadness, but I realize I'm not going to argue with him. I'm sorry, Mum; I'm sorry, Dad; I'm sorry, Nanny and Granddad; I'm sorry, Uncle Richard, Auntie Yetta; I'm sorry, Mum's friends; I'm sorry, our old neighbours; I'm sorry, all the people outside synagogue on Yom Kippur; I'm sorry, my Sunday school teachers; I'm sorry, Abraham; I'm sorry, Moses; I'm sorry, Judas Maccabeus; I'm sorry, Anatoly Shcharansky; I'm sorry, Anne Frank; I'm sorry, Golda Meir; I'm sorry, the Reform Synagogues of Great Britain; and I'm sorry, the *Jewish Chronicle*. I'm sorry, and I love you, but I can't.

I understand, as I haven't before, that my son and I have grown up in different realities: in mine, it was self-evident that the children of Jewish women were themselves Jews; in his, Jewishness denotes religious affiliation, something that can be freely refused. And besides, how can he be wholly Jewish when he is half his father's child? That defies logic. That defies *maths*.

Perhaps he will change his mind one day, but I realize that I don't have the heart to insist that he change it for my sake, or his late grandmother's, or the Patriarchs', or even – the definitive last words of my upbringing – for the sake of the victims of the Holocaust. I may have given him life, but it is *his life now*.

⁎⁎

The last time I saw Julian in the flesh, he was walking forward, and away, towards the passport control desk at Heathrow. It was late December 2004. He had come to visit us in Cambridge, where he had met his nephew for the first and last time, and then we had all spent Christmas with Mum in Stanmore. She was standing next to me crying and I was trying to console her. I don't remember exactly what I said – probably that there'd be plenty of other opportunities to meet again, plenty more visits.

In my mind's eye, Julian often has his back to me. I try to call him, to get him to turn round and let me talk him out of going, or at least tell me why he must, but he never does.

**

They may be gone, my brother and my mother, but that doesn't end my relationships with them. I remain, as my therapist put it, 'enmeshed', all tangled up in the family hoard. This book has been both a continuation of my conversations with them, and an attempt to untangle myself.

That's futile, probably. The dreams I've had since their deaths would suggest so.

I dream that Mum phones. We have a conversation which is utterly unremarkable in every way, except that when I ask her how she is, she says, matter-of-factly, 'I'm dead.' I know she is, and discover that before she died she paid for a service which recorded her voice saying all the typical phrases she'd use in her daily conversation with me, and then left them several thousand pounds to pay in advance for the voice to call me at 6 o'clock every day, until such time as the credit runs out. I decide that while this might be irritating and a little creepy, I can cope with it, though it's hard to say whether she's doing this to look after me or keep tabs on me from beyond the grave. But when I discover that she's also paid them to animate her corpse, so that it lumbers after me at bus stops even while it's decomposing, I am scared and horrified and try to get it to go back to its corpse home as soon as possible.

．：

Another time I dream about Julian as well as Mum. I realize – and their shades tell me – that I am having very strong hallucinations. I want them to go away, so I try to banish them as if they are dreams, but the images have too much solidity and reality for me to do this. They dare me to get rid of them, but I can't.

And my relationship with my brother's image is not so bad, really; in between my attempts to banish him, we talk about my state of mind, his death, our childhood. His age keeps changing. Sometimes he's twelve. Another time, I see an image of him in early adulthood on the other side of a large, full-length mirror. I walk towards the image and it approaches me. We talk to each other from opposite sides of the mirror, but neither of us can cross.

．：

I was lucky to have had him, lucky to have had a brother close in age who was happy to play with me, to share jokes, or to make things together.

I was an odd child: solemn, precocious and awkward with my peers. Although I was never entirely without friends, I would often find myself alone in the infant school playground, and when my year moved from the infants' up into the junior school, the classes were shuffled and my isolation increased. I formed a friendship with another outsider in my class, a girl who was academically able, like me, but also disabled, which meant that she was often absent for treatment, and when she was I would be alone again, and would be sent to the back of the dinner line because I couldn't find a partner. Often I would tell my mother I didn't feel well enough to go to school. My new friend's mother suggested to mine that she take me to see an educational psychologist. She did, and I was diagnosed as 'gifted'; it was still the 1970s, when there were no other diagnoses available for solemn, precocious, awkward children.

At the psychologist's suggestion my parents joined the National Association for Gifted Children, and took me along to a club the association ran on Saturday afternoons in Kilburn, where children could engage in activities they enjoyed and be precocious together without fear of mockery. As a sibling of a Gifted Child, my brother was allowed to come too. He may well have qualified on his own account, but he always had friends at school, so nobody thought of testing him.

When we started at the club, my brother was put in a younger age group, so we always spent the afternoon apart, but after a couple of years he was moved up and we would sometimes sign up for the same activities. One Saturday we both opted for three woodwork sessions. The teacher showed the two of us an oblong piece of plywood the size of a desktop and suggested that if we worked as a team, we could, in the space of one afternoon, make a real table, something we could take home and use.

We were very excited at the thought of making our own furniture, and for three hours the two of us worked steadily together. We took turns to do the more satisfying jobs, the sawing and hammering; we took turns to hold the wood steady while the other one did the interesting work. Under the guidance of the woodwork teacher, we found four leg pieces, sawed and planed them down to the right size, screwed them to the table top, sawed and planed four flatter pieces into a skirt to support the legs, attached them at the corners and to the table top, then stood back and marvelled. The table came home with us and stood in my bedroom for some years, until one day I (or was it one of my friends?) sat on it, and the table top, which was never meant to be sat on, broke in half. We had no use for any of the other parts and they were all thrown away. I was upset about it then and I'm heartbroken now. It really was the world's most perfect table.

∴

Look: I've found a way for Julian to help me not-quite-finish this work. I've decided to give him the last word on our childhood.

Chris and I were married at the Cambridge registry office on Saturday 26 August 2000, with Julian as one of the witnesses.

There were very few people present at the ceremony, but we held a big reception on the Sunday, when the more religious members of our family and my mother's more Orthodox friends were able to travel. Our Uncle Richard arrived with his camcorder and made us a DVD, so I still have a record of the speech my brother made when he welcomed everyone to the reception, taking the place of our late father.

Julian: *Thank you from Joanne and Chris's mother – on behalf of –* (Our mother says something. He looks at her and shrugs. She says something again.) *I'm getting criticized in the first sentence!* (My voice, from off-screen left: *Carry on.*) *Heckled by my mother! So – on behalf of my mother, and Chris's mother Pat, I'd like to welcome you to the wedding of Joanne and Chris, even though the wedding was actually yesterday and, as a witness, I can say that it did actually happen and they are actually married* (Laughter. Off-screen, Chris and I hold up our left hands, and Julian points at us.) *– there are the rings to prove it.*

So I'd like to thank everybody for making it here today, especially those of you who've had to travel a long distance. I know there are people who've come here from Germany, from Israel, and apparently there's someone here from San Francisco… (Laughter.) *There are a few people who couldn't make it and will obviously be missed, and I especially want to mention Chris's brother Pete and his sister Jan and their families, who are in New Zealand, which is obviously a long way for them to come. We should also all take a moment to remember Chris's father Ken, Joanne's and my father Maurice as well as our Aunt Marian and our grandparents who have all sadly passed on. I think their spirits, wherever they are, are smiling on this occasion, and I think Dad would have been tickled pink to have met Chris because he's everything that he wanted Joanne's husband to be: he can cook, he can clean, and does all the ironing.* (Very loud laughter.)

So I… I was actually the first person to hear the news that Joanne and Chris were gonna get married. I heard by email. I think that Joanne just wanted to tell somebody – she couldn't tell anybody else before she told (He points to our mother.) *Mum and Pat, so I was the only person who was, you know, a long way away, and I was told not to tell anybody, but I was very, very excited when I heard the news and I couldn't contain myself, so I told all my friends in Connecticut as soon as I found out, and I think that my excitement really shows the wonderful relationship that Joanne and I enjoy now, but… erm… it hasn't always been that way.* (Pause.)

So, when we were very young, there was a certain amount of animosity between us. From my point of view, most of the animosity went this way. (Points to me, then towards himself. Laughter.) *Of course, a lot of you know that Joanne cut up my security blanket.* (An uneasy noise, not really laughter, more a collective intake of breath. My uncle chooses this point to go in for a close-up of Julian.) *She used to hit me, and she buried the evidence that she hit me, and the evidence in this case was an audiotape that was made when I was eighteen months* (Looks towards me for confirmation.) *and Joanne would've been three and a half. We had one of those old cigar-shaped… cigar-box-shaped tape recorders when they first came out. And Mum and Dad decided to make a tape of Joanne and me being young, for posterity. And at one point there's this moment of silence, followed by a young boy crying, when you hear Dad say, 'Joanne! What did you hit Julian for?* (Laughter.) *Ruth! Ruth!*

Joanne's hit Julian! What should I do?' (Loud laughter. He pauses, and smiles.) *And I think that pretty well sums up most of our childhood.* (He's looking at me and grinning.)

But the real reason that the tape was buried was not because of that. It was because there was a one-off recording of Joanne singing Jimmy Osmond's 'Long-Haired Lover from Liverpool'. I did try and find the tape, but it was too deeply buried in the back garden, so you're all spared that today.

But the abuse wasn't all one-way traffic, I have to say, and we used to have a climbing frame in the back garden, it was one of those coloured metal ones, and I would've been about two years old, and I was climbing the climbing frame naked – as you do when you're two, and I needed to answer a call of nature. I was a long way up, it was a long way down, I felt free and easy so I just went – and I honestly didn't know that Joanne was down there. (Laughter.) *But it does allow me to say that I've literally pissed on my sister from a great height.* (More laughter. He giggles, then recovers himself.)

Later that day our Aunt Marian came round with Nikki and Lisa and they were supposed to take Joanne out to the pictures, but she was late, with the excuse that (Adopts small child's voice.) *'Julian weed on me,' an excuse I have to say she hasn't been able to use since then.* (Close-up of me smiling at him.)

But now that we're all grown up I have to say that I respect Joanne, I like Joanne, I love Joanne (I pull a self-conscious face.) *and I live 6,000 miles away from Joanne* (I laugh.) *– and our relationship has never been better. It's something we clearly share with Chris's family, who like him so much they all moved to New Zealand – which brings me on to welcome*

Chris and Pat to our family. We're honoured and very, very happy to count you among our number now, and Chris, I feel lucky to have someone as nice as you as an in-law, and they say you can't choose your family – in this case Joanne was choosing for us, and she couldn't have chosen any better, and I've never seen her as settled or as happy as she's been since they've been going out together, and over the months I can genuinely say that I've come to regard you as someone whose presence I can tolerate for short periods. (Chris: *That's beautiful.*) *Thank you.*

So I'd like to wish you and Joanne many, many happy years together – I think everyone would like to do that, and I'd also like to wish you lots and lots of babies – that's Mum's bit there… So, ladies and gentlemen, we know you have a choice of weddings to go to, we'd like to thank you for joining the wedding of Chris and Joanne, and I also have to point out that there are disposable cameras on the table (Kerry, Chris's Best Person, says something to him.)*… There are? There aren't. There should have been disposable cameras on the tables, but never mind – when they arrive, please feel free to dispose of them. Please, everybody, enjoy yourselves and – welcome. Thank you.* (Much applause.)

*

Santorini, 2014. We land at Thira at eleven on a cool, spring night. As I get out of the plane, a fresh breeze slaps the last of the diazepam out of my system; I'm going to be awake and alert for hours. Never mind.

The airport is tiny; it takes one short, tight corridor to get to passport control and no time at all to get through it. That takes us straight into baggage claim, where our suitcase is already waiting, inside it the photo album I have made for Giselle. Now there's one more corner, one more tiny corridor, and then we'll see them – they must be on the other side of this wall. There's no time to arrange my face or decide how I feel.

But they've been here for hours. They'll have had time to get nervous, to wonder what we'll be like, to wonder, even, if we're really coming. That must be worse.

I see my sister-in-law first, so I wave and call out, and trip over our suitcase. Never mind.

My niece is standing in front of her mother. She is wearing a white dress, an embroidered pink cardigan and a pair of sparkly bunny ears.

'She's been so excited to meet you,' Ayako says. 'She's been saying "Where are they? Where are they? Is that them now? When are they coming?"'

But now she's gone quiet. She smiles and stares. Her eyes are the same shape as mine and my brother's, but their own colour, and huge. My son – whose eyes are the same shape again but the colour of his father's – goes up to her and holds out his hand.

'High five!' he says. She does, and then they start talking.

**

It is not for you to complete the work, but you are not free to idle from it.

Acknowledgements

This was not an easy book to write, and I am very grateful for the help and support I have received. *Small Pieces* began its life as a PhD project, and many thanks are due to my supervisor, Dr Meg Jensen, for all her advice and guidance. Polly Clark has been, as always, a wonderful first reader. I would also like to thank my agent, Louise Greenberg, as well as Karen Duffy and Sam Brown at Atlantic Books. The rabbis who feature in the introduction to the book are real, and I am grateful to them for the answers they gave to my questions, and for introducing me to *Pirkei Avot*. My husband Chris and my cousins Lisa and Nikki also appear as themselves, and deserve much thanks for all the support they've given to me over the years, and for being generous readers of the book. My sister-in-law, who chose the pseudonyms I've used for her and for my niece, has been especially kind in her response to *Small Pieces*. I am aware always that although we all have our own versions, very few of us are able to publish them. I hope I have made good use of the privilege. Thank you all.